Elizabeth Ilive,
Egremont's Countess

Elizabeth Ilive, Egremont's Countess

c. 1769 - 1822

Sheila Haines, Leigh Lawson & Alison McCann

Elizabeth Ilive, Egremont's Countess
First published in 2017 by Bakehouse Press.

Set in Monotype Fournier 185.
Designed and produced by Jonathan Newdick
and printed and bound in England by the
Lavenham Press.

ISBN 978-1-9997421-0-2

Front cover. A detail from Thomas Phillips, *Elizabeth Ilive in a blue and white turban*, oil on canvas, 134.6 × 106.7 cm. Collins Baker Catalogue No 504, courtesy of The National Trust.

Opposite. Thomas Phillips, *Elizabeth Ilive*, '*Mrs. Wyndham*', oil on canvas, 1799, 125.5 × 100 cm. Collins Baker Catalogue No 564. Private Collection, courtesy of Lord Egremont. Elizabeth here is portrayed with her diagram of the award winning improved cross bar lever, the RSA silver medal awarded to her for the lever and an open copy of RSA *Transactions*. (See pages 41 to 45).

FSC

Acknowledgements

The authors would like to thank Lord Egremont for allowing us to use the Petworth House Archives; Father Edward Jackman and the Jackman Foundation for their generous support; Jennifer Thomas for her help and suggestions in editing the text; Andrew Loukes of the National Trust at Petworth House for his long-term support; Wendy Cameron and Brenda Dougall Merriman for advice on the text; Elinor Gallant and Jo Gallant for sending us images of Elizabeth Ilive and Thomas Hamilton Ayliffe belonging to their family; Anne Monk, Ayliffe family historian, for her invaluable help and encouragement; Jeremy Masters for sharing his Ayliffe research and Martin Frost, for drawing the map.

We would also like to thank the following institutions for allowing us to use their archives: Bodleian Library; Brighton Local Studies Library; British Library; City of Westminster Archives; Foundling Museum; Isle of Wight Record Office; London Metropolitan Archives; Oxfordshire Record Office; Royal Academy Library; Royal Society of Arts; Somerset Archives; Somerset Archaeological & Natural History Collection; Staffordshire County Record Office; Surrey History Centre; University of Sussex; Wellcome Institute Library; Westminster School Archives; West Sussex Record Office.

The following people have all been of assistance for which we are very grateful: Diane Ladlow, Alan Redman and Clare Snoad (all West Sussex Record Office); Kathy Chester; Graham Jaunay; Leslie Tomas Miller; Jane Monk; Marie Murphy (Secretary of the General Cemetery Company, Kensal Green); Janet Payne (Society of Apothecaries); Anne-Marie Purcell (Hammersmith and Fulham Local Studies and Archives); Phil Spain (Ramsgate History on-line); Carrie Starren (Hurlingham Club Archives); the Vicar of St. Decuman's, Watchet for showing us the Wyndham Memorials in 2009; Eve Watson (Royal Society of Arts) and Georgina Duncan, secretary to Lord Egremont.

Finally, heartfelt thanks are due to Jonathan Newdick for his help and advice and for designing the book.

A NOTE ON CURRENCY
Prior to 1971, the UK's currency consisted of pounds (£), shillings (s) and pence (d), £1. 8s. 4d. for example, means one pound, eight shillings and four pence. There were twelve pence in a shilling and twenty shillings in a pound. A guinea was twenty-one shillings, or £1. 1s.

Contents

Preface

After the publication of our biography of the Reverend Thomas Sockett of Petworth in 2007, Sheila Haines wanted me to work with her again – this time on a biography of Elizabeth Ilive, long-term mistress and, eventually, wife to George O'Brien Wyndham, 3rd Earl of Egremont.

Because of Elizabeth's interest in science and the award of a silver medal from the Royal Society of Arts for her invention of an improved cross-bar lever, this intriguingly unconventional mistress was of particular appeal to Sheila. There was also the connection that Thomas Sockett, before his ordination, had been tutor at Petworth House to the illegitimate sons of Elizabeth and the Earl.

We met every week to discuss and work on our project and went on regular research trips together, then, tragically, in 2011, Sheila became ill and learned that she had only a few months to live. Despite this devastating news and fighting increasing frailty, Sheila was determined to begin drafting the text and footnotes. However there were still several aspects waiting to be covered, not least the important question of Elizabeth's parentage. We had explored many ideas and suggestions in our endeavour to solve that mystery – but without success and Sheila decided she would write without confirming Elizabeth's identity and background.

Sheila asked Alison McCann, Petworth House Archivist, if she would assist me in completing the text and footnotes. We have done this to the best of our ability, making use of Sheila's copious notes. We are very grateful for editorial advice from Jennifer Thomas.

I am also grateful to have had additional suggestions and encouragement from Anne Monk in Australia, a descendant of Elizabeth's brother Thomas. Only days before Sheila's death, Anne contacted me to say that she had found Elizabeth Ilive's silver medal for sale in England on the internet. She had bought the medal and it was still with her daughter in London. With some drama we managed to bring the medal down to Sussex and Sheila actually held it in her hand. This was an incredibly moving and significant moment as the silver medal had always been foremost in Sheila's mind and she often hoped that it would one day turn up in some forgotten drawer. The medal has since made a public appearance at an exhibition at Petworth House. Anne has been a great help tracking down additional material on the internet and we are extremely thankful for her expertise and co-operation.

We have been able to incorporate other exciting new material which, sadly, was discovered too late for Sheila to know about. Just a few months later, on a research trip to Oxford, Alison and I found a petition from Abraham Ilive in *Jackson's Oxford Journal* which confirmed the name of Elizabeth's father. This confirmation has also been found by another Australian Ayliffe descendant, Jeremy Masters, who, we now realise, has been researching his ancestors at the same time as ourselves. We are grateful to him for sending us copies of his recent treatise on the Ilive/Ayliffe family – and we are pleased to be able to include some interesting sources that he discovered.

We offer this completed work as a tribute to Sheila and acknowledge, with grateful thanks, Father Edward Jackman and the Jackman Foundation of Toronto for their continued support of the project. Whilst making the changes and additions to the text that needed to be made, we have tried to ensure that this is very much Sheila's work, in her own style, reflecting her own particular interests.

LEIGH LAWSON

BROADWATER,

WORTHING, WEST SUSSEX

The 3rd Earl of Egremont

To put Elizabeth's story in context, here follows a brief description of the man whose life she shared for so many years.

George Wyndham, later 3rd Earl of Egremont was born in 1751, the eldest son of Charles Wyndham 2nd Earl of Egremont. His father was Secretary of State for the Southern Department; his mother Alicia Maria Carpenter, a noted beauty. The young Lord Cockermouth, as he was known, was sent to Pampellone's School* and then to Westminster. In 1763 the 2nd Earl died, and the twelve year old boy inherited the vast family estates, comprising some 120,000 acres in Sussex, Somerset, Yorkshire and Cumberland. From school he went to Christ Church Oxford, accompanied by the Reverend Euseby Cleaver, later Archbishop of Dublin, as his personal tutor. In 1770, the Earl embarked on a Grand Tour, visiting Dresden; Berlin; Prague; Frankfurt and Paris and returning with Meissen porcelain; lace; champagne and Tokay. From his next Grand Tour in around 1772 he returned with Mlle du Thé, a French actress, to whom he was so faithfully devoted that his family were said to be worried that he might marry her. A match was arranged for him with Lady Maria Waldegrave in 1780, but the Earl persuaded her to cancel the engagement, because he was afraid that he would not make her a good husband. In about 1786, he started a relationship with the woman who was to be his longest lasting and acknowledged mistress, Elizabeth Ilive, but

*A fashionable school in Wandsworth run by M. Pampellone, a Frenchman. Charles James Fox was also a pupil there.

it was by no means an exclusive relationship.

As a very wealthy peer, the Earl took his place in the highest society, with its amoral, louche and extravagant habits. His friends included Lady Melbourne (two of whose children he was said to have fathered) the Duchess of Devonshire and Charles James Fox, as well as the Prince Regent, with whom he shared a mistress, Elizabeth Fox. He was one of the Macaroni set, who wore extravagant fashions, but he was reported not to drink to excess and did not indulge in the fashionable vice of gambling.

He gradually developed other interests. He became a great patron of art, especially of contemporary British artists and sculptors. Most notable among these was J.M.W. Turner, but the Earl's country house, Petworth in Sussex, was visited by many different artists, who could look for inspiration to the extensive collection of works of art that had been gathered by the Earl's ancestors.

The Earl was interested in agriculture, and the possibilities for improvement. He was a member of the Board of Agriculture and corresponded with Arthur Young. He carried out experiments in crop and stock raising on his Sussex estates, introduced there a new form of plough from Suffolk, and turned part of his deer park into a model farm. He was also involved in the setting up of local Agricultural Societies. He was a successful breeder of racehorses, and winner of five Derbies and five Oaks. *

The Earl was immensely wealthy, and also extremely generous to charitable causes. He sponsored hospitals, schools, and almshouses and supported numerous societies for the improvement of the lot of the less

---

* The Derby Stakes run at Epsom Down, Surrey; inaugurated in 1780; won by the Earl in 1782, 1804, 1805, 1807 and 1826. The Oaks run at Epsom Down, inaugurated in 1779; won by the Earl in 1788, 1789, 1795, 1800 and 1820.

George O'Brien Wyndham, mezzotint, W. Derby/H. Robinson published by John Phillips 1 September 1828. WSRO, Castle Goring PD 92.

fortunate. He was a supporter of Edward Jenner, and arranged for the inoculation of people on his estates against smallpox. He sponsored the Petworth Emigration Scheme, which sent emigrants to Canada from his Sussex estates, under far better conditions than most emigrants experienced. He invested in projects to build canals and improve rivers and roads, thus helping the local economy and giving employment to local people. He built new cottages on his estates, gave a 'bounty' of clothes and food to the deserving poor and towards the end of his long life, gave a huge party for his birthday each year, to which the people on his estates were invited with their families. George Greville described the 1834 feast in his diary. Six thousand people were fed and

> Nothing could exceed the pleasure of that fine old fellow; he was in and out of the windows of his room twenty times enjoying the sight of these poor wretches attired in their best cramming themselves and their brats with as much as they could devour, and snatching a day of relaxation and happiness.[1]

The Earl was also generous to friends and artists, lending or giving money. Shortly before he died, he burnt a lot of promissory notes so that those who owed him money would not be bothered after his death. The burning of most of his personal papers by his executors unfortunately means that a potential source of information about his relationships with the people around him was destroyed.

He did not take part in national politics, though he was identified with the Whigs when younger, but became more Tory as he grew older. In his own county, he served as a magistrate, and as Lord Lieutenant from 1819 to 1835.

He lived to a very great age, still active despite frequent attacks of problems with his trachea, which seem to have afflicted him each winter. When he died in 1837, the local and national newspapers mourned the passing of a great philanthropist and forty artists followed his coffin.

ALISON MCCANN, ARCHIVIST TO LORD EGREMONT

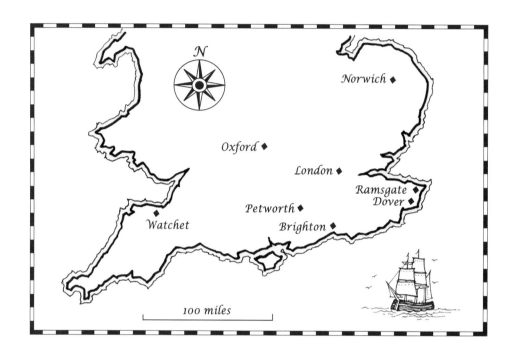

Map to indicate the main places associated with Elizabeth Ilive.
Drawn by Martin Frost.

1. *Mrs. Wyndham and 'all the Younger Branches'*

'She was neither desirous of being married to His Lordship nor of being acknowledged Countess of Egremont...'[2] wrote Farington. It does seem extremely careless, given the Egremont title and quantities of Egremont land and money at stake, that Elizabeth Ilive and Lord Egremont were together for fourteen years and in that time had seven illegitimate children over a space of nine years before they eventually married. The Earl certainly had many other illegitimate children, some of whom he had acknowledged to the extent of accepting some financial responsibility for them, and some of whom he did not. However, it was only Elizabeth's children who carried the family name of Wyndham. They were brought up at Petworth as his own, together with Mary Fox, one of his children by Eliza Fox alias Crole. It was Elizabeth Ilive who lived at Petworth and in London as his Lady. She may not have wanted to marry him but, given the fact that the Earl of Egremont could have practically anyone he chose as a mistress, and did, she possibly also appealed to him as a personable and intelligent young woman.

She was reputed to have been 'very beautiful and very innocent'[3] when she met his Lordship at fifteen years of age but the first factual reference we have to her is when George, her first child by the Earl of Egremont, was baptised at St. Marylebone Church on 22nd July 1787 as 'George Wyndham the son of George and Elizabeth, born 5th June'.[4] The information on her proposed memorial,[5] illustrated on page 99, suggests that Elizabeth was born in 1769 and she would, therefore, have been sixteen or seventeen when George was conceived.

It may be that marriage was never on the agenda at the beginning of their relationship. Elizabeth was desirable and so was the Earl. He was, at thirty-six, an immensely rich, worldly-wise, autocratic, irascible, but generous peer. Marriage, as an institution, was a very different arrangement from a love affair. Lord Egremont was a close friend of the Prince of Wales and moved around in the highest aristocratic circles where a desirable mistress was a separate acquisition from a wife.

Elizabeth's roots and family history were shrouded in mystery, but she was certainly far below the Earl in social status and therefore unacceptable as a wife in the eyes of society. There may have been few known facts but there was certainly plenty of speculation at the time and since. Elizabeth has been cited in a variety of sources: as the daughter of a Devon farmer;[6] of a master at Westminster School;[7] as the daughter of the Reverend Iliffe, a Surrey clergyman, possibly the vicar of Bramley, who reputedly practically sold her over to the Earl of Egremont 'when quite young';[8] or as a descendant of the Irish Hamilton family.[9] The artist, Ozias Humphrey* said, he 'believed she was a farmer's daughter',[10] although the Earl was reported to have asked on occasion whether 'little H[umphry] talked as much nonsense as ever.'[11]

Correspondence, many years later, in the *Western Times* of June-July 1886 only added further confusion.[12] An article in *Truth* magazine had raised questions about the Earl's marriage. The *Western Times* asked if there were any traditions on the Devon estates of the Earl having married the daughter of a 'Scotch or North Country' farmer. A correspondent replied with details of 'a legend which was extant on the Egremont estates in a bygone generation'. According to the legend, the Earl had married the daughter of a North Country or Scottish farmer, there had been issue

*Ozias Humphrey (1742-1810) miniature and portrait painter.

Illustration from *The Genealogy of the most Ancient and Noble Family of Wyndham...*
by William Radclyffe, Rouge Croix Pursuivant of Arms, 1819 and continued to the year
1821. Private collection, courtesy of Lord Egremont, reproduced here at actual size.

of the marriage, and 'the lady quitted the Earl rather abruptly.' Another correspondent added to this that Elizabeth Ilive, his countess, had left him, having discovered that he had been privately married before.

Our recent research has finally confirmed some of the details given by William Radclyffe, a herald of somewhat dubious credentials at the College of Arms, in the sumptuously hand painted and gilded genealogy of the Wyndham family that he compiled in 1819.[13]

He stated that Elizabeth was the third daughter of Abraham Ilive and Cecilia, his wife. Radclyffe further stated that Cecilia was the daughter of Col. O'Dorighty, by Cecilia, his wife, the sister of James John Hamilton of Dunnamanna Co. Tyrone. In general, Radclyffe's information makes Elizabeth's family background sound as if it is of gentry status. This was not necessarily the truth: what is certain is that the Ilive family were printers, and Elizabeth's mother was probably Irish. With no record of the marriage yet found, we cannot confirm that Cecilia's maiden name was O'Dorighty.

Elizabeth had a brother, Thomas Ilive, who trained as an apothecary[14] with John Gabb. It was through Thomas's apprenticeship that the name of their father was, at last, confirmed. Thomas later added a second name, Hamilton, and used the variant spelling Ayliffe, although he still called himself Thomas Ilive in 1802 when he was listed in a London street directory.[15] On his apprenticeship papers in 1789, he was described as the son of Abraham Ilive of Oxford, who had died in 1777.[16]

Abraham Ilive of Oxford was a printer, related to a well-known family of printers and during his final illness a petition for financial support was made in *Jackson's Oxford Journal* on his behalf.[17] The petition, printed on 24th January 1777, stated that Abraham was the great grandson of Dr. Thomas James,* and that his father and brothers were all printers but were now long since dead:

Sir Robert Peat (1772-1837), *Portrait of Mr. Thomas Hamilton Ayliffe Surgeon*, tempera (?) on board, 7 × 6 cm., reproduced here actual size. Private collection, courtesy of Elinor Gallant and Jo Gallant.

* Thomas James was appointed the librarian of the Bodleian Library 13 April 1602. He was actually the great-great grandfather of Abraham. Thomas James married Anne Underhill in Oxford; they had seven children, one of whom, Francis James, was Abraham's grandfather.

... your Petitioner ... is now 74 Years of Age, confined to his Bed by
a severe Fit of Illness, has a Wife and four Children, and in want of
the common Necessaries of Life ... he begs leave to submit his Case to
the Gentlemen of the University ... such as are inclined to assist this
distressed old Man and his helpless Family ...

That Abraham needed financial help with his children indicates that, despite
his advanced years, they were quite young and not adults of working age.
'Abraham Iliver' was buried at St. Thomas', Oxford on 30th January 1777,
so he did not live for more than a few days after the petition was published.
The Pension Lists of the Stationers' Company record that Mrs. Cecilia Ilive
received a pension of 10s. 6d. a quarter from 1777 until 1800.[18] Did the
family ever receive assistance from the Gentlemen of the University as a result
of their heartfelt petition? Possibly not, because despite the small pension from
the Stationer's Company, Cecilia Ilive had returned to her husband's home
parish of St. Botolph without Aldersgate in London by June 1778 and was
recorded as an inmate of the parish workhouse there.[19] Perhaps she was ill and
unable to support her children. As Elizabeth and Thomas were under eight years
of age at that time, they may have been in the workhouse with her, but they are
not named. The family was evidently still in need of assistance because Cecilia's
older daughter Frances, then aged 'about nineteen years' was examined in the
Register of Orders of the parish of St. Clement Danes, London on 5th June
1778 on behalf of her sister Maria, aged 'about thirteen years'. This was for the
settlement of Maria in the parish of St. Botolph without Aldersgate, to which
parish she was duly removed on the same day.[20] Her removal from one parish
to the other was required because her father, Abraham Ilive, had 'Rented and
lived in a House called London house in Aldersgate street for several years ...'[21]
Indeed, he had been baptised in that parish on 25th September 1706.[22] It

To the Rev. the Vice Chancellor, Heads of Houses, and other Members of the University of Oxford,

The Petition of ABRAHAM ILIVE,

Great Grandson to Dr. THOMAS JAMES,

Cotemporary with Sir *Thomas Bodley* and Mr. *Camden*, and who published the first Catalogue of the Bodleian Library,

HUMBLY SHEWETH,

THAT your Petitioner, who is a Printer, and whose Father and Brothers were all bred to the same Business, and long since dead, is now 74 Years of Age, confined to his Bed by a severe Fit of Illness, has a Wife and four Children, and in want of the common Necessaries of Life. — Under these deplorable Circumstances, he begs Leave to submit his Case to the Gentlemen of the University, from whose known Humanity he hopes to receive that Assistance he stands in need of.

And your Petitioner, as in Duty bound, will ever pray, &c.

Such as are inclined to assist this distressed old Man and his helpless Family, are requested to leave their Donations with Mr. D. Prince, Bookseller; Mr. W. Jackson, Printer, High-Street; at Baggs', Dick's, Horseman's, and Tom's Coffee-Houses; at the Cross Inn, in the Corn-Market; the Wheat-Sheaf and Anchor, in St. Aldates; or at the University Printing-House, where the Truth of the above will be attested.

OXFORD, 24th January, 1777.

Petition, *Jackson's Oxford Journal* 25 Jan 1777 p. 3. By permission of the British Library and Oxfordshire History Centre.

was in this examination that Frances stated that her mother was 'now in the workhouse belonging to St. Botolph without Aldersgate...'[23] Perhaps if a traditional family story is true, it was then that Elizabeth was taken to a convent in France, but if so, by whom and where did the finances come from? Neither is it known who funded the apprenticeship of Thomas.

If she was still living in the workhouse several years later, Cecilia may not have been aware that Elizabeth was cohabiting with the wealthy Earl of Egremont and had borne him several children. Perhaps her children did not try to keep in touch with her or help her for some reason. Had she known, surely she must have hoped for financial assistance from her daughter, after all, Elizabeth helped to support her brother, but there is no evidence of any aid forthcoming. There is no mention of Cecilia in Petworth House Archives, yet she probably did not die until at least 1800 when she was last recorded in receipt of the Stationers Company pension, just a year before Elizabeth finally married the Earl. However, the register of the poor in the parish workhouse of St. Botolph without Aldersgate contains a discharge entry for one Cesele Iliff on 29th September 1791.[24] If this was indeed Cecilia Ilive, perhaps she was rescued from a workhouse existence by her children.

Despite the unfortunate start to their young lives, the Ilive girls did extraordinarily well for themselves. Apart from Elizabeth's success, one of the sisters, either Frances or Maria, according to family lore married a member of the McLeod family[25] and the other married Colonel Meade,[26] who is cited at the time of Elizabeth's death as her brother-in-law.[27] No marriage or other records have yet been found to clarify or confirm this information.

Elizabeth and Lord Egremont would not have moved in the same social circles. George's baptism at St. Marylebone and their later history suggests that they probably met in London, where, perhaps, Elizabeth had gone with her family when they returned in 1778 to their father's last place of settlement. By the time George was born they were committed enough for the Earl to give the baby the name of Wyndham. If the Earl attended the baptism he could have maintained a prudent presence in the church as there were twenty-two babies baptised on the same day, possibly at one ceremony.[28] Their daughter Frances, known as Frances Wyndham, born in 1789, was to encounter problems over her surname nineteen years later when she was to marry Charles Burrell. The Earl was suddenly fraught about the legal validity of their forthcoming marriage. Should the banns be called in her accepted name of Frances Wyndham, or as William Tyler* was at pains to explain to the Earl, in her legal name of Frances Ilive? Perhaps the banns had better be called in both names if there was doubt. In any event, the marriage settlement had to be corrected throughout from Wyndham to Ilive.[29]

Henry, the second son, was born in 1790 when Elizabeth was twenty. She now begins to appear in the Petworth House Archives with the courtesy title of Mrs. Wyndham.[30] Her first visit to the grand Sussex mansion, the marble hall, magnificent stables and grounds must have been an awe-inspiring experience, and her presence as a settled resident and mother must have been ambivalent. The Earl's mother, the second Countess of Egremont and previous mistress of the house, had married again and was living elsewhere, but Elizabeth's position was informal and unstable and the long-standing servants and workforce for which Petworth House was well known, would have taken it as such.

Another new member of the household in 1790 was William André, the surgeon, one of a family notable in the medical profession. As there was now a nursery at Petworth, it was desirable to have a medical man to hand. He not only looked after the health of the babies, but also of members of the

* William Tyler, agent to the Earl from 1801 to 1835.

household and people from the town referred to him by the Earl. A surgery was built for him in the house in 1790.[31]

There was to be another informal branch of the Wyndham family by 1792. Mary Fox was the daughter of the Earl of Egremont and Eliza Fox. Eliza was the daughter of Joseph Fox, a part-time actor, theatre manager and tavern-keeper in Bow Street, Covent Garden. Eliza appeared on stage at the Haymarket theatre and Drury Lane. She was also known by the courtesy title of Mrs. Crole and as a mistress of the Prince of Wales.[32]

Joseph Fox brought parties of actors for summer seasons at the theatres in Brighton and Lewes in the 1780s and 1790s.[33] The Earl of Egremont had boxes in all the fashionable London theatres.[34] He had a house in Brighton and was often in Brighton or Lewes for the races. Mary was not the only child of Eliza Fox to be recognised by the Earl as his. In 1795 he made a settlement of an annuity of three per cent on £13,333 for Elizabeth Fox (Crole) and her children Charles Richard, aged eighteen months or 'thereabouts' and Mary, aged three 'or thereabouts'.[35] In a later will of about 1800, he added in William Crole 'now at Mrs. Daw's Preparatory School at Turnham Green' and Anne Crole at 'Mrs. Edbridge's School in Kennington'.[36] But Mary was the only one to be brought up at Petworth with his acknowledged family.

Eliza Crole may have unwittingly been the cause of the death of Elizabeth's two sons Edward Wyndham Ilive, born and dying in 1792, and William Wyndham Ilive born in August 1793 to die in February 1794.[37] Children did die in considerable numbers from a variety of causes but there is no evidence from the Petworth burial records of a grouping of infant deaths from any local epidemic. Syphilis was rife at all levels of society in the eighteenth century and the Earl was sharing Eliza Crole with the Prince of Wales, a well-known chronic sufferer from the disease. Indeed, the Earl may have been suffering from syphilis before this time, it being a well known result of the aristocratic young man's Grand Tour when he brought home syphilis along with his French and Italian art treasures. The Earl of Egremont did two European tours between 1770 and 1772. Had he been affected, the Earl might have taken a cure and been clear when he took up with Elizabeth or it might be that the syphilis, as it could, skipped Elizabeth's first three children, only to resurface with the fourth and fifth – with fatal consequences.[38] One can only imagine the feelings of Elizabeth and the effect on her relationship with the Earl if this was the case.

The deaths of little Edward and William affected their parents 'much' as William Hayley the poet records. Hayley was godfather to William, his namesake, and had been affected by the 'tender circumstances' of William's baptism at Petworth in September 1793. In February 1794 the Earl visited Hayley in great distress and burst into tears in his library telling him of the baby's death. Elizabeth and the other children stayed at Eartham with Hayley until after the funeral.[39]

The next babies to be born were Charlotte in 1795 and Charles in 1796. As Elizabeth was not moving in society and seldom went to London she was dependent on Petworth House for interest and occupation and there was a great deal of life both in the House and flowing in and out of the great estate. Her children provided one increasing and demanding source of life and amusement. In the autumn of 1795 on his annual visit to Hayley, George Romney, the fashionable portrait painter, at the Earl's request and with Hayley's encouragement, went up to Petworth from Eartham and began a portrait of Elizabeth and the children, to be known as Titania with her fairies, though later catalogued as *The Egremont Family*:[40]

Some to kill cankers in the musk-rose buds;
Some war with rere-mice for their leathern wings,

The Egremont Family, George
Romney, oil on canvas,
168.9 × 228.6 cm. Collins
Baker No 381. Private collection,
courtesy of Lord Egremont,
Matthew Hollow Photography.

To make my small elves coats; and some keep back

The clamourous owl . . .[41]

Romney had a penchant for portraying his models as Shakespearean characters; he had painted Hayley's son, Thomas Alphonso, as Puck in 1792 and throughout the 1790s produced a number of pictures and sketches around the theme of A Midsummer Night's Dream.

Unlike Titania, in this picture, Elizabeth, in sea green, is a far from ethereal queen of the fairies. She appears recumbent and rather beaten down by the substantial fairies gathered around her. George in scarlet and Henry, do indeed, have bows and arrows and are shooting at bats, the rere-mice, but these fairies will need to shoot a great many bats to make themselves leathern jackets. Frances, in white muslin, appropriately carries a garland of flowers. Charlotte, a few months old, is clasped in her mother's arms and clutching her hair. There does not appear to be an owl. Romney finished the picture in August 1796 but did not change the overall original design. By this time Charlotte was no longer a small baby and Elizabeth was heavily pregnant with Charles.

A nurse and several nursemaids were responsible for the day and night care of the children but Elizabeth was responsible for ordering and arranging the education and playtime of her children. The household accounts, some of them in Elizabeth's name, give a detailed picture of their nursery life and early education. When Farington wrote in his diary 'Lord Egremont keeps a lady and has several children'[42] this was doubtless literally true; the bills may have been in Elizabeth's name but the Earl ultimately paid them. It was unlikely that Elizabeth had money of her own; her brother, Thomas, was constantly in financial trouble and eventually went bankrupt. In the early days of Elizabeth and the Earl's relationship it may be he handed out money when he wished, but Elizabeth might have had a regular allowance. Certainly, some of the bills specifically say 'paid by Mrs. Wyndham', suggesting she personally had the cash or resources to do so.[43]

With Elizabeth's ordering and the Earl's money, the nursery schoolroom was well equipped. There were dissected maps – in effect, jigsaw puzzles – of England, Asia, America and Africa; maps of England and Europe, reflecting the contemporary interest in exploration and mapping of the world; a dissected alphabet; sets of ivory letters; a pence table*; copybooks, slates and pencils for early writing lessons.[44] The children learned to read from Anna Letitia Barbauld's* best-selling *Lessons for Children*.[45] These little sixpenny books were published from 1778 onwards and it may be that Elizabeth had learned to read from them herself; it has been suggested that probably three-fourths of the gentry of three generations learned to read from Barbauld's books.[46] These were not the fairy stories or legends of earlier chapbooks* produced for children but realistic, simple lessons based in true enlightened fashion on the observations and everyday life of one little boy, Charles.

> The task is humble but not mean; for to lay the first stone of a noble building, and to plant the first idea in a human mind can be no dishonour to any hand.[47]

Barbauld's Lessons, with their rational and mundane approach, came under attack for depriving children of imaginative and fantastic legends and

---

* A pence table is an arithmetical table for easy conversion of pounds and shillings into pence and vice versa.
* Anna Letitia Barbauld (1743-1825) was an innovative children's writer. She had a successful writing career, and was a poet and teacher.
* A chapbook is a cheap paper-bound book, used for more ephemeral works such as children's books.

stories. Charles Lamb wrote irately to Coleridge:

> *Goody Two Shoes* is almost out of print. Mrs. Barbauld's stuff has
> banished all the old classics of the nursery... Science has succeeded
> Poetry no less in the little walks of children than with men.[48]

The Wyndham children did have storybooks: one such, *A Cabinet of
Lilliput*, was a collection of ten or twelve little volumes of stories each with
an illustration, in a small case.[49] However, these were still highly moral and
instructive stories with titles such as 'Good Behaviour to Servants', 'Indolence
Reclaimed' and 'Industry of the Ant'.[50] Early lessons for the children were
probably given by their mother and nursery staff. Later, James Goldring,
the master of the local Taylor Charity School and his own boarding school
and owner of the local printing and stationery business, submitted accounts
for materials and for giving the children lessons.[51] By 1797, if not before,
they had a governess.[52] Other specialist teachers taught skills suitable for
an earl's children: French grammar and exercises; broadsword lessons for
George and Henry; and dancing lessons for both boys and girls.[53] Well-
educated young ladies were expected to be able to dance, play the piano
– Frances had piano lessons – and sketch. Elizabeth herself owned she took
great pleasure in painting and devoted much of her time to it. Quantities of
prepared paper, bottles of colours, pencils, brushes and varnish came down
from London in 1796 for her use, and later, for both mother and daughters.
There were also models of the anatomy of the horse and human figure.[54]

Petworth House, its grounds and gardens, provided wide scope for fun
and games. There was a skittle alley[55] and 'managery' with rabbits, guinea
pigs, a parrot and other birds,[56] and a silk wormery.[57] The lake provided
opportunity for boating and fishing, and skating in the winter. The estate

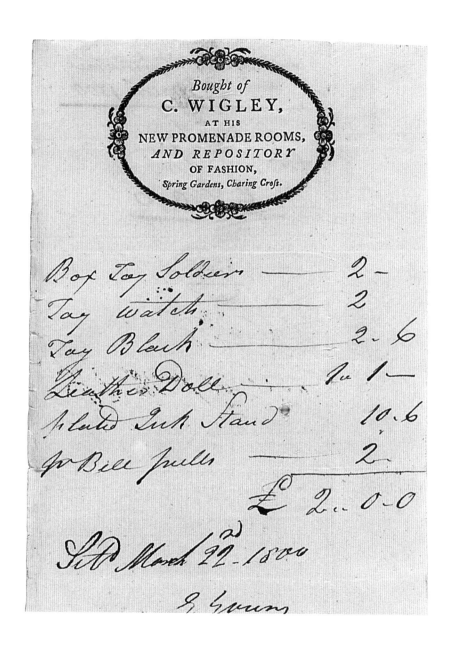

Bought of
C. WIGLEY,
AT HIS
NEW PROMENADE ROOMS,
AND REPOSITORY
OF FASHION,
Spring Gardens, Charing Cross.

Box Toy Soldiers	2 -
Toy watch	2
Toy Black	2 . 6
Leather Doll	1 -
Plated Ink Stand	10 . 6
pr Bill Pulls	2 -
£	2 . 0 - 0

Setd March 22 - 1800

S Evans

Bill from C. Wigley 'at his new promenade rooms and repository of fashion, Spring Gardens Charing Cross', PHA 8064.

35

carpenters made a playhouse with miniature furniture; a chair for the great doll; a swing in the pleasure grounds; a cart and garden rake for Master George; and they mended a rocking horse for Charles. There were dolls, toy soldiers and a horn for Henry.[58] The stables and horses were an important facet of Petworth life. The children had riding lessons. They could see their father's splendid race horses and foals, and the spectacle of the hunt departing almost every day during the season. Elizabeth's riding would have been curtailed by her pregnancies but after Charles' birth in 1796 there were no more babies for six years and she and the children rode for pleasure and perhaps took part in the hunting. In 1800, for riding, Elizabeth had a new 'fine blue ladies Cloth habit, & Pettic[oa]t' – the latter being the skirt of the habit containing '3 breadths' of material – with a 'long train, a bl[ac]k Velvet Collar Silk Sleeve lining' and gilt buttons. Frances, now eleven, had a habit similar to her mother's but without the train; the youngest Miss Wyndham, Charlotte, had a fine scarlet cloth greatcoat made as a habit.[59]

The Petworth House Archives contain a quantity of bills for clothes and accessories bought by Elizabeth from shops in fashionable New Bond Street and Piccadilly. Many of the children's clothes would have been made at home

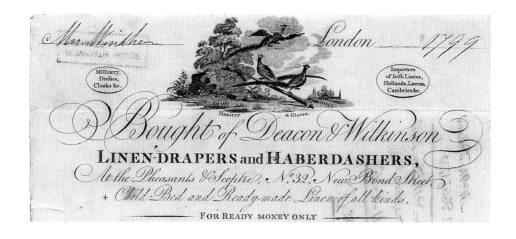

by the nursery staff or the seamstress employed by the House. Elizabeth bought yards and yards of white muslin from C. Deacon in Piccadilly, much of it intended for the babies' and girls' simple dresses. B. Smallwood, at The Golden Ball, Hanover Square, haberdashers, supplied lambs' wool, and whalebone knitting needles; warm woollies would be welcome over thin muslin. Elizabeth, Charlotte and Frances had purple shoes made of kidskin or dogskin by Thomas Ellis, and straw summer hats from Lee and Co, 6, New Bond Street. For winter, the girls had fine cloth greatcoats with black velvet collars and gilt buttons made by Winter, Shee and Winter, who had made the riding habits. This firm also made boys' and men's wear but that did not appear to be Elizabeth's territory.[60]

Bills from Winter Shee and Winter, PHA 8082 (above) and from Deacon & Wilkinson (opposite), linen drapers and haberdashers, 'at the Pheasant & Sceptre, No 32 New Bond Street, London', PHA 8064.

2. *The Inventress and Female Cultivator*

It may be the loss of the two baby boys in 1793 and 1794 that spurred Elizabeth into another part of her life and, perhaps, the people around her encouraged this as one way of coping with her sorrow and loss. In 1795, between the arrival of Charlotte and that of Charles eighteen months later, she was occupied with a project of her own. In October she wrote a letter to Samuel More,* the Secretary of the Royal Society for the encouragement of Arts, Manufactures and Commerce (known as the RSA) at the Adelphi in London; 'I am very much obliged to you for the great variety of seeds which you have been so good as to give me and in return I have sent you a model of a mechanical invention of my own which you will laugh at as every body did here at first'.[61]

Her letter to Samuel More has a diffident opening. Who was laughing at her at Petworth and whom did she expect would laugh at the Adelphi? It was, perhaps, an indication of her ambivalent position at Petworth as the mistress of Lord Egremont but, seemingly, not the Mistress of the House. Additionally, she was exceeding the expectations of her as a woman, regarding the things that women did and did not do. The laughter might percolate from the Earl and his friends, down through the servants into the kitchen and out to the men in the fields, stables and yards. It also echoed

---

* Samuel More (1726-99) apothecary and administrator; elected a member of the Society of Arts, Manufacturers and Commerce in 1761; elected secretary in 1770 and re-elected each year until his death.

down the years. In 1908 her grandson, Percy Wyndham, dismissively spoke of her as 'affecting science as her hobby to the extent that Lord Egremont got the Royal Society to give her a medal for some pamphlet she had written.' [62] Who would be laughing at the RSA?

If More was laughing it would be kindly laughter. A friend and advisor to the Earl of Egremont, he was a frequent visitor to Petworth during his extensive travels nationwide. He knew Elizabeth and the 'Younger Branches' [63] in the nursery and the seeds he had given her for her garden, were possibly rare ones from the collections of his friend, Joseph Banks. An apothecary by training, More became a renowned, respected and popular figure amongst the great and good of the scientific and industrial world. He had been Secretary of the RSA for twenty-seven years and lived with his wife above the Society's premises at the Adelphi in John Adams Street.

Women appeared seldom in the lists of prizes offered yearly by the Society from its foundation in 1754. The names of the few, as might be expected, appeared in the Polite Arts section. However, the invention Elizabeth submitted came under the scrutiny of the Mechanicks Committee: no woman had won a medal in this section before. The Committee had an unusual task. One might imagine the bemused, perhaps indulgent, perhaps disapproving, men who gathered in January 1796 to consider her application for the acknowledgement of her invention of an improved cross-bar lever for the use of the workmen on the Petworth Estate.

Given the laughter, she might never have applied. Perhaps she did not take laughter to heart, or had often laughed companionably with More, or cheerfully at herself, but it mattered enough for her to start her correspondence with acknowledgement of it. Nevertheless, she was strong-minded enough to persist but was not without help and support. At Petworth House there was a little group of people interested in scientific, philosophical and contemporary ideas – William André, the surgeon; Robert Ferryman, the naturalist; John Boultbee, the animal painter; Benjamin Arnold, the music master; Thomas Sockett, the Rector, who had an early interest in electricity and, of course, the Earl himself. The estate carpenters prepared the 'Philosopher's Room' which was probably where scientific experiments were carried out.[64] Elizabeth was apparently the only female member of this group, but there were other women nationwide, including the so-called 'Blue Stockings' (like Anna Letitia Barbauld) well-known for their enlightened interest in science, philosophy and literature.

The latest 'Proceedings' of learned and influential institutions and societies, of which the Earl was usually a member, were to be found on the shelves at the London house and at Petworth House and men of note in political, cultural and agricultural affairs came and went. Samuel More may have actively encouraged Elizabeth to apply to the RSA and Arthur Young, a life member of the Society, probably did so, as well. Young,[65] who was the Secretary to the Board of Agriculture, was another frequent visitor to Petworth, an admirer and promoter of the agricultural innovation and research undertaken by the Earl of Egremont. He was also a friend and admirer of Elizabeth, commenting on her excellent disposition and good sense. He brought her equipment for the laboratory installed in the House and taught her how to use it.[66] Other practical help came from the carpenters who made the innovative cross-bar lever and a model of it, to go to London with Elizabeth's letter.[67] They may have laughed as they did so, circumspectly. They may not have laughed at all but been impressed, as Elizabeth wrote, 'I assure you it has proved of great use and the workmen all approve of it very much.'[68]

She may also have been encouraged by other applications from men in the Petworth area.[69] In the same year, John Upton, woodward and carpenter to the Earl of Egremont, submitted plans to the Mechanicks Committee for a hollow, moveable threshing floor. Another local man, Richard Eager of Graffham, had invented a 'simple yet effectual method' of relieving cattle and sheep who were 'hoven' or blown from over-eating clover, rape or 'turneps'. The Earl of Egremont sent letters supporting the entries of Upton and Eager but did not do so for Elizabeth. It was possibly not politic, nor socially 'done' that he should.

Elizabeth's description to More of the production of her invention makes it clear that she followed a proper scientific method. She observed, suggested, tried and formally wrote up the results;

> Since you left Petworth a great work has begun of moving earth in which there are great quarries of stone and I observed that the men made use of the lever in a very ineffectual manner by standing three and four at a time on the bar of the lever by which means they were placed so near the fulcrum that their power was lost besides that they were obliged to steady themselves upon sticks for fear of falling which took off from their weight upon the lever.[70]

Her suggestion was the addition of a 'cross-bar for the workmen to hold by' and another at the opposite end for the men to stand on 'when the strength of the rocks require an increase of power.' By this means, their concentrated weight increased the force of the lever and ensured the safety of the men, who no longer needed to balance themselves with sticks. Did her suggestion come after knowledgeable consideration of the physical principles behind the working of a lever and its fulcrum that she had acquired in her earlier education? The physical sciences did not usually play a part in the education of women. Or did she perhaps look at the situation with common sense and

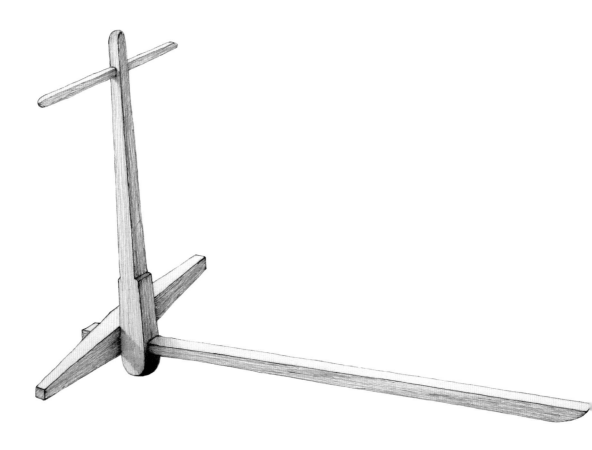

Elizabeth Ilive's design for the Cross-Bar Lever. Drawn by Jonathan Newdick after a diagram in the Royal Society of Arts *Transactions*, 1796, 2295-2298.

see what might be done and how, then, put into practice?

The model sent to the Society had a neatly labelled diagram outlining the principle on which the lever worked but Elizabeth was prudent, adding a little justifiable, truthful flattery, at the end of her letter to More; 'I wish I could prevail upon you to come here and look at it and I dare say that your great knowledge would suggest some improvement.' [71] She signed her letter 'Elizabeth Ilive' and then overwrote Ilive by 'Wyndham'. Did she like her own name and cling to it, or did someone suggest that Wyndham would carry more weight with the RSA?

The Mechanicks Committee met on 4th February 1796 to take into consideration the model of the Cross-Bar Lever and to read Elizabeth's letter. They resolved that her invention was new and ingenious and recommended that they present their Silver Medal to the Inventress, Mrs. Wyndham, a resolution that was confirmed in the usual way by a ballot taken on 17th

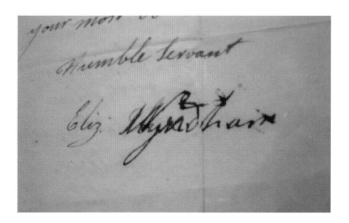

Elizabeth's signature altered from Ilive to Wyndham, letter to the Royal Society of Arts dated 1796.

February. The Silver Medal also carried a prize of twenty guineas. The model lever was to be kept at the RSA for inspection, if desired. Unfortunately, it was not still there for inspection in 2009, but a replica was made for the National Trust at Petworth House in 2012.

The prize giving was on Tuesday 31st May 1796 at the Society's house at the Adelphi. Elizabeth did not go. 'I am very sorry that the present state of my health will not allow me to have the honor of attending the meeting'[72] Charles, her fifth son and seventh child, was born in the late summer of 1796, so her pregnancy would have precluded her attendance. It seemed accepted practice that women did attend and went up to the platform to collect their prizes. Mrs. Barbauld went to such a prize-giving in 1805 or 1806 and wrote:

> as there are few occasions on which a young lady has to exhibit herself as an object of public attention, I could not help feeling greatly interested for the females who with palpitating hearts, were to receive the reward of their talents.[73]

Samuel More accepted Elizabeth's prize on her behalf. She apologised for giving him so much trouble and requested him 'to express to the Society the high sense which I entertain of the honor which they have conferred upon me!' Mr. Upton was to take the medal, inscribed 'TO M^{RS} WYNDHAM MDCCXCVI N^{O}. CLXX CROSS BAR LEVER IMPROVED', back with him to Petworth. As she was not married, the twenty guineas belonged to her. She possibly invested it in her next project, for the cross-bar lever was not Elizabeth's only scientific interest in 1796. She wrote to the RSA 'I hope this year to be able to send you an accurate experiment of the culture of potatoes from shoots'.[74]

The cultivation of potatoes was an interest the RSA, in common with other agricultural and scientific institutions, actively promoted in the second half of the 1790s. This interest was spurred by the war with France and the difficulty of importing wheat from the continent, coupled with the bad harvests at home of the late 1790s. The price of wheat rose from an average of forty-nine shillings a quarter in 1790 to one hundred shillings a quarter* by 1805. There were riots over the price of bread, the staple of the labourers' diet. These riots were disturbing in themselves but also frightening in the context of the revolution taking place in France. It was not only labourers who suffered. The staff at Petworth House and the London house were severely rationed. Tyler grumbled that the 1801 bill for bread at the London house 'is enormous...nobody at Petworth except at his Lordship's own table is allowed Bread at his expense.'[75]

* A 'quarter' is a quarter of a hundredweight. i.e. 28 lbs.

Opposite. RSA Silver Medal won by Mrs. Wyndham for her 'Cross Bar Lever Improved', 1796. By T. Pingo, designed by James Stuart. Brittania, seated, is conferred with honours by Mercury and Minerva. Diameter 44mm. Our own photograph by permission of Anne Monk.

Potatoes had been hitherto used both as feed for overwintering livestock and a staple diet for the desperately poor. Potatoes were eaten at the Petworth House dinner table but only as an occasional vegetable. The Petworth gardeners raised Fine Early Champion forcing potatoes, middle crop and main crop kidney potatoes later in the summer for use in the kitchen and to store over winter.[76] English people, in general, were not urged to take to potatoes for subsistence, but to consider rice pudding and parsnips as alternatives to bread. Young recommended the Earl to consider importing rice and cited the town of Wymondham in Norfolk, which had done so and sold it to local people at tuppence a pound.[77] The most pressing perceived need for improvement in potato cultivation was for cheap fodder for fattening livestock and feeding them through the winter, in place of scarce, expensive grain.

Elizabeth had organised small experiments on potato growing in 1795 after the birth of Charlotte, but embarked on a properly organised trial in the early spring of 1796, having dispatched her work on the lever to the RSA. For £6, she rented six and a half acres of rough farmland – there being apparently none to spare for free on the Petworth estate. Here Elizabeth embarked on a trial of planting one quarter of an acre with pieces of the coarse, large, red, cluster potato, each containing one or two eyes. Another five and a half acres were planted with shoots stripped from the yellow Ox-noble potato. Both varieties could be stored over the winter and were used as animal food. The potato pieces were planted nine inches apart, in rows; one quarter acre of shoots were dibbled in vertically; and the remaining shoots were planted lengthwise end to end in trenches taken out by a hoe. To begin with, these shoots were each about one foot long at planting, but when the supply began to run short the remainder were cut into two inch pieces also planted horizontally but nine inches apart.

Although Elizabeth writes 'I planted', 'I dibbled', the labour force was supplied by local men and children. The six bushel of red cluster potatoes with eyes were cut into suitable pieces by old people, and 'the expense not attended to'. These were then planted by one man and four children who planted the quarter acre in a day. The man earned 1s. 6d., the standard day's pay for an agricultural labourer, the children, perhaps his own, earned 6d each.

Dibbling in shoots of the Ox-noble potatoes was very troublesome and expensive and the labour cost £1.3s.6d: around fifteen day's work for the man on his own, or a week for the team of one man and four children. It was quicker to plant the shoots, one to one and a half feet long, end to end, in drills drawn out by men with a hoe. The children followed the trenches with their baskets and dropped shoots into the drills so quickly that, unless the men had begun to draw out the drills the day before, the children overtook them and were forced to stand still to give the men more time. Elizabeth noted a plough would have been quicker and cost less. The men then had to follow behind the children and cover over the drills. Between May and August, weeding and earthing-up was undertaken by a man with a hoe, the children doing those tasks by hand. The crop was harvested in October when the men dug the potatoes and the children loaded them into carts.

The trial was hampered by cold weather in February. The dibbled shoots, the tops of which protruded above the ground, suffered from cold wind and frost – one fears the children did, too. Elizabeth acknowledged it had been too early to plant, but she had needed to remove the shoots from the overwintered potatoes by then and had not realised she could store shoots on their own, in pits, until a later suitable planting time. Weeds in the largely uncleaned land were troublesome later in the spring: especially avena, false oat grass, which flourishes in rough ground. The dibbled plants and the small shoots in drills were largely suffocated by weeds. The eyes did reasonably well but the long potato shoots grown in drills were the pride of the trial. They sprouted from every joint and 'the whole length of the drills were regularly filled with plants and potatoes.' Elizabeth commented that the success of the shoots was doubly pleasing in that they were usually stripped from the potatoes and discarded.

The total expense of the experiment was £20.11s.9d., which might have taken nearly all of her silver medal guineas. Nevertheless, the crop of 1,676 bushels of potatoes valued in the market at one shilling a bushel would yield £83.16s., a good return on her money – if that money were actually realised in a sale. There is no record of Elizabeth sending a report of this experiment to the RSA or doing further trials, as Young had suggested she might when he printed her report in his *Annals of Agriculture* in March 1797.[78] He had visited Petworth in June 1796 whilst the trial was underway and may have then suggested to Elizabeth that he would publish her results in his journal. In any event, there was to be trouble.

Young always referred to the Earl in terms of great respect, giving due honour to his title. Nevertheless, he wrote a spirited and irritable letter to 'My Lord' when the Earl forbade Elizabeth's name to be put to the published article:

> I rec[eive]d both your very obliging favours. I should have been still more so had you not been so firm ag[ains]t the name appearing. I confess that I am very far from being convinced. Of what consequence to a careful reader, the age, sex, or beauty of a writer, provided he or she writes good Sense? I know these scruples are all your Lordships, because when I saw Mrs. Wyndham she consented that her name should be annexed, but observed that perhaps you would not approve it: but I cannot see any distinction between very ingeniously inventing a lever or with equal ingenuity experimenting on potatoes.[79]

Elizabeth had seemingly been aware that the Earl would object. The issue of undesirable publicity had been forestalled with the RSA by Elizabeth's pregnancy. Her name was given in their printed *Transactions*, but perhaps the Earl felt the readership of these would be limited and socially acceptable compared to the readership of the *Annals*, intended for landowners and farmers in general.

Young suggests that the scruples felt by the Earl centred not only on her sex but also on her youth and beauty. Young openly admired Elizabeth and the Earl may have been resentful of Young's encouragement of her scientific interests, his tendresse toward her and his admiration of her intelligent good sense.

The contemporary debate between the qualities of sense, seen as a desirable male attribute and sensibility as a female attribute, or perhaps weakness, was very much in the air. On one occasion, Young wrote to the Earl from Exeter with comments about a young woman at a dinner party who 'talked much of France' so that, to his dismay, he scarcely got a word in edgeways. He comments, 'If Mrs. Wyndham does not understand this as a complement to her I shall take it ill'.[80] This implies Elizabeth's ability to talk intelligently as well as listen to others in a discussion.

Young gave the Earl a chance to relax his severity, as he had already sent the manuscript to the printers with Elizabeth's name added to it, 'knowing I could strike that out if you forbid its appearing'.[81] It was forbidden. Young did his best to counteract the censorship by heading the article 'Planting Potato Shoots by a Lady', naming 'Petworth' as the site of the trial, and adding a final paragraph of his own:

It is with great pleasure I insert this very interesting paper. It is highly satisfactory, and proves clearly that the method detailed is of real importance; and as this very ingenious lady intends prosecuting her trials next year in a field better prepared for the experiment, I have no doubt but she will command a yet more brilliant success, and establish so beneficial a practice free from every doubt and hesitation; indeed the result of the present trial goes nearly to do this. I could enlarge here on the merit of attending to such objects – but the reflections must be obvious to every reader. When female cultivators can thus form and register their experiments, it is with reason I wish for more such correspondents.[82]

Young hints that Elizabeth might have been given better land at the outset. He does, however, go out of his way to placate the Earl, asking as a favour if he can also print a paper written by the Earl himself.

The winter of 1796/97 was very cold whilst Elizabeth was preoccupied with baby Charles and writing up her report on potatoes, but life was not all earnest. In addition to the learned journals coming into Petworth House, there were fashion magazines: *The Gallery of Fashion* and *Bayles' Register of Fashion*.[83] This winter Elizabeth had two new greatcoats from S. Taniere: one brown sarsenet (fine, soft, silk) wadded and lined with pink silk and trimmed with brown fur; the other purple sarsenet wadded and lined with silk and trimmed with swansdown. With them, she wore a black velvet bonnet and a swansdown ruff. The account rendered from the London fashion house was for £17.00.[84] The greatcoats were the newest fashion in London but did not take long to spread to the provinces. Mrs. Custance and her eldest daughter, the family of Squire Custance of Norfolk, called on Parson Woodforde, who noted in his diary in November 1800 'They were very fashionably dressed. Mrs. Custance & eldest Daughter were dressed in brown Silk Pellises, or Great-Coats'.[85] Silk was expensive but very much in fashion, given the contemporary rage for all things Chinese.

London 25th March 1800

Bo.t of R. Robinson late Mr.

James Summersett,

Wholesale & Retail

LINEN-DRAPER, MERCER and HOSIER,

At the SUN, 62 Broad Street, Bloomsbury, 3 Doors from the Top of Drury Lane.
Sells Flannels, Blankets, Counterpanes, Bed Ticks, Thicksetts, Velveteens, Corderoys,
Ready made Shirts &c &c &c.

Bill from R Robinson, late Mr. James Somersett, linen draper and hosier 'at The Sun, 62 Broad Street, Bloomsbury, 3 doors from the Top of Drury Lane', London, PHA 8084/57.

3. *A Great Delight in Painting and Scientific Learning*

The pattern of life in the nursery was broken when George, aged eight, was removed from his mother's and nursery care and sent away to school in nearby Midhurst. Life was stringent at boarding schools in the eighteenth century. George was not happy, took fever and was sent home, with his head shaved, to be nursed back to health. When he was well, he made a scene, sobbing bitterly at the prospect of going back to the dreaded school.[86]

It may have been Elizabeth, it could have been the Earl, who, weakened by George's misery, and looking for alternatives, consulted Hayley. On their visits to Eartham they had been much impressed with little Thomas Alphonso, Hayley's son by his housekeeper, Mary Cockerell.[87] Thomas Alphonso, taught by his father, had started to learn Latin at four and Greek at five. Hayley, who had had a miserable experience himself at boarding school in Kingston, Surrey, took pity on George. He offered to take him as a pupil and boarder in his house at Eartham; and, incidentally, was probably glad of the money.[88] George was happy to go: he had known Hayley and Thomas Alphonso for years and, given the coming and going between Eartham and Petworth, was not cut off from home. Hayley was building a villa at Felpham on the Sussex coast and so there were also visits to the seaside and bathing.

Hayley did not undertake George's education on his own, for at Eartham there was young Thomas Sockett, another protégé of Hayley's, who had been living with him since 1792 when he came as companion-cum-tutor to Thomas Alphonso. Sockett, the son of an impoverished London bookseller,* was ten years older than George and had already met him on visits to and from Petworth House. He was intelligent, had been taught Latin by his father, or at school, and learned Greek with Thomas Alphonso. He and George did lessons together with Hayley from 1795 to 1797, with a break when Sockett was away working on Edward Gibbon's memoirs with Lord Sheffield at Sheffield Park.[89]

By 1797 Thomas Alphonso was increasingly ill with tuberculosis of the spine. Hayley decided he could not care for his son and teach George so proposed sending him home again to Petworth. George was greatly upset at the recurring possibility of being sent away to school and relieved and thankful when his parents decided to keep him at Petworth and educate their children at home.

Thomas Sockett, now twenty, was highly recommended as a suitable tutor by Hayley, who stressed:

the great advantage which George has derived from the industry and intelligence of Mr. Sockett. He is a young man, who to a strong understanding adds a grateful heart, and whom I zealously recommend to the favour of your Lordship, not only on his own account but on that of his younger fellow student.[90]

Mr. Sockett moved into the schoolroom at Petworth House in May 1797 and undertook the formal education of George and Henry, an education based on learning Latin and Greek, with some French and German and reading from classical texts.[91] Informally, there was widespread educational activity in and around the House and grounds.

Sockett would have enjoyed this and he became an enthusiastic member

* The Sockett family business was in Cloth Fair, off Aldersgate Street, where Thomas was born in 1777. Thomas Sockett was later to become Rector of Petworth, the Earl having arranged for his ordination in the Church of England.

of the little scientific coterie at Petworth. He was to be interested all his life in scientific and technological research and development. The Earl may not have wished Elizabeth to pursue her scientific studies in the public eye but he was willing to finance her interests at Petworth. With their decision to employ Sockett and educate the children at home there were additional spurs to encourage interest in the contemporary world of practical and scientific studies. The Earl himself was a leading figure in the world of agricultural research and technological innovation and had become a member of the new Board of Agriculture in 1793. Sockett had been introduced to Hayley when, as a young lad, he had shown skill in the use of the electrical shock machine – a device which manually produced electrical shock waves, used both as a medical treatment and a source of amusement. The Earl had bought two such machines and an 'electric chair' in 1779 and 1780.[92]

From 1797 the interest of the philosophic group turned to chemistry: an interest popular in philosophic and pragmatic circles nationwide, fostered by the work of Priestley and Lavoisier,* into the nature of elements and the understanding of their importance as the building blocks of the material world. This was shown in practice by the increasing number of businesses supplying experimental equipment. A laboratory was set up at Petworth House which resulted in the purchase of a portable chest of chemicals plus quantities of equipment and materials bought in London, often by Arthur Young and dispatched by carrier to Petworth. Falwasser, a Chemist and Druggist, at 19 Haymarket, Holt, at 51 Haymarket and Johanne Hempel of

---

* Joseph Priestly (1733-1804) theologian, natural philosopher, chemist and educator. Credited with the discovery of opxygen.
Antoine Levoisier (1743-94) French nobleman and chemist, most noted for discovering the role oxygen plays in combustion. Guillotined in the French Revolution.

Scientific equipment used by Elizabeth Ilive at Petworth House. Our own photograph courtesy of Lord Egremont.

Kings Road, Chelsea supplied retorts, crucibles, phials, scales and weights. Falwasser sold chemical materials including volatile caustic alkali, iron filings, lead, and brass wire. Wedgewood and Byerley supplied a thermometer and Joshua Peckover an iron furnace from the Norwich Iron Foundry. This latter might have been a small furnace for laboratory use or a larger one for use in the smithy, making a plough following Young's instructions.[93]

Young also promised to teach Elizabeth how to weigh hydrostatically; there were books which would give instructions on how to weigh powders lighter than water, but face to face instruction would probably be better. Mr. Blount, the optician, had had a specification from Young and would supply a hydrostatic balance and thermometers.

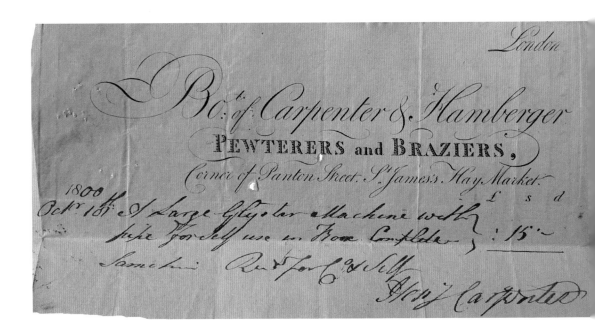

Bill from Carpenter & Hamberger, pewterers and braziers, 'corner of Panton Street, St. James's, Hay Market', London, PHA 8064.

I also mean to propose to her a small stage near her window for a few pots to feed plants with infammable [*sic*] air* and I have an apparatus in Suffolk which I will send for against spring for sowing in.[94]

The glyster machine ordered from Carpenter and Hamberger[95] may have been for André to use in its intended function to administer enemas but Humphry Davy,* the chemist and inventor, was said to use an old glyster machine along with sundry kitchen utensils as experimental equipment. Perhaps the Petworth group did so too. André was a member and he may well have been kept busy binding up other members' wounds when experiments went wrong. We do not know how much the children were encouraged to participate in experiments, but they may have done so.

The Earl of Egremont was not always sanguine about practical chemistry:

I was fool enough to remit to . . . the chymist . . . and get six gallons of Mr. Davies mixture to accelerate vegetation and I steeped all my turnip seed in it and the consequence is that not one seed has vegetated and I have the trouble of sowing a hundred acres over again. So for my share of the experiment.[96]

Chemistry, however, was not the only interest. In 1798 the Earl paid John Russell for a lunar globe, a selenographic instrument for studying the surface of the moon and other astronomical instruments.[97] A camera obscura, from J. Ramsden, and a model telegraph were set up in the grounds. The museum

* 'inflammable air' was a term used for hydrogen gas.
* Sir Humphry Davy (1778-1829) was awarded the Rumford medal in 1816 for his miners' safety lamp.

in Petworth House, in the care of the Reverend Robert Ferryman,* was enriched with models of sheep and cattle.[98]

André, as well as providing first aid and caring for the health of the House and town in his dispensary, was responsible for implementing the new procedure of smallpox vaccination. Writing to the Earl in 1789, Edward Jenner outlined the debate going on in medical circles over the effectiveness of smallpox versus cowpox vaccine. By 1796 the Earl was on the Board of the Hospital for Smallpox and Inoculation in London; by 1803 he was a member of the Royal Jennerian Association. The efficacy of cowpox vaccine was widely accepted by 1805. Jenner had visited the Earl and in a letter expressed the hope of seeing him again in London to 'talk about a plan to offer vaccination to the poor of the metropolis'.[99] He had met Mrs. Wyndham on his visit and sent her his best respects. André's involvement was to be recorded on his tombstone by the Earl; 'to his professional skill hundreds have been indebted for health and life.'

Whilst such earnest, enlightened, scientific learning and rational experimentation was going on at Petworth, it was increasingly being counterbalanced by events over the channel. At its beginning in 1789, the French Revolution was regarded positively by many British people. However, when Louis XVI was executed in 1793 and the news spread of the horrors of the Terror, public opinion in Great Britain began to change. 'What a picture of madness and folly in all parties' Sockett was to comment later in his Journal.[100] The news coming from Paris was brought home in very real fashion by the French refugees arriving on the south coast of England. Aristocratic mansions, including Sheffield Park and Petworth

* Revd Robert Ferryman (1752-1837) clergyman, museum keeper, missionary, inventor, set up a private museum at Petworth House from c. 1796-1802. It appears to have been composed largely of stuffed birds and animals.

House, offered succour and hospitality to members of the French aristocracy, now impoverished and homeless. English ladies took refugees under their wing: Young's wife, Martha, sought Elizabeth's aid for the plight of de Salis, an émigré and 'a real object of pity', who had been imprisoned in York Castle and liberated on payment of £28. The Youngs invited him to stay in their London lodgings before he started work as a bailiff for Lord Sheffield. Mrs. Young hoped to call at Petworth and 'introduce herself to Mrs. Wyndham.'[101]

Elizabeth seems, from this extract from Farington's diaries, to have been impressed by the attitude of some of the émigrés and compared it to the disadvantage of the English lord:

> Mrs. Wyndham who lives with Lord Egremont called on me to see my pictures. I told her I had none finished by me but hoped in a few months to have several to shew her. She professed to have great delight in painting and devotes much of her time to it. Mr. André, the Surgeon, she said, lives with them and had mentioned me as had Philips. She had a fine little Boy with her, abt. 2 years old, very like Lord Egremont. She spoke warmly in favor of Monsr. Calonne, said He was an enthusiast in regard to pictures, and much of a gentleman in manners. She remarked on the little impression the great changes in France seem to have made on his mind, as on other of the Emigrants, who instead of breaking their hearts as Englishmen wd. do, from being Counts turn Cobblers or anything for a livelihood.[102]

Elizabeth, apparently, could not envisage the Earl of Egremont becoming a cobbler out of necessity.

Charles Alexandre, Vicomte de Calonne was a poverty-struck émigré statesman. He had been a minister to Louis XIV and fell out of favour over his fiscal policy. He came to England between 1787 and 1789 and again after 1790, visiting Petworth House. There was a considerable traffic in valuable art collections across the Channel before and after the outbreak of the French revolution. Calonne sold his valuable collection of pictures by auction in London in 1795 to pay debts incurred by his personal extravagance and his support for the beleaguered French nobility. The sale took four days and included works by renowned French, Italian and Flemish artists. Elizabeth evidently liked Calonne, and the Earl paid Phillips, the portrait painter, seven guineas for a portrait of him in 1799.[103]

Farington also noted:

> She invited me to Petworth, and said Ld. Egremont wd. be glad to see me there. She seldom comes to town, not oftener than once a year, but thinks she shall come in the Spring to see the Orleans collection which I mentioned to her – She appears to be abt. 36 years old.[104]

The Orleans Collection, that Elizabeth intended to view, was another great collection of French and Italian art sold by the ill-starred Philippe D'Orleans* in 1793. It had made its way to London via Brussels where it was eventually purchased by a group of three noblemen, headed by the Duke of Bridgewater, for £43,500. The exhibition they organised in London, at galleries in Pall Mall and the Strand, from the end of December 1798 offered some of the pictures for sale by private deal. Ninety-four of the paintings were marked for retention by members of the syndicate. The remainder were, eventually, auctioned from the end of January 1800. Elizabeth would have had to pay

* Phillipe D'Orleans Duke of Orleans (1747-93) a supporter of the French Revolution; sold the magnificent art collection of his predecessor Phillipe D'Orleans (d. 1723). He was guillotined in 1793.

2s. 6d entrance fee to the exhibition, which was a fashionable and financial great occasion. Over all, the syndicate made an enormous profit from their enterprise.

Farington suggests that Elizabeth was about thirty-six years old when, in fact, she was only twenty-eight. He may not have been good at estimating ages but Elizabeth had been ill at the beginning of the year: perhaps this and the advent of seven children in nine years had aged her or, perhaps, on this December day, Charles had tired her – although he would probably have had a nursemaid with him. In 1798, the Wyndham nursemaids included Sarah Collins, Sarah Cooper and Ann Manson.[105] André was to order syrup of poppies for Elizabeth from William Pirner, the London apothecary, in 1799 and in 1803, her footman, John Stedman, included 'lodnum' in his expenses on Elizabeth's behalf.[106] However, in the eighteenth century and much of the nineteenth, opium in one form or another was freely available and women would have taken it in much the same way as a twenty-first century woman would resort to aspirin or paracetamol.

One less traumatic but significant influence from France was the introduction of the empire line in women's fashion: fine cotton muslin dresses in a classical style, usually white, short-sleeved, high-waisted, tied under the breast with a sash, with no train but a simple hem at the bottom. Elizabeth had nine such 'round' dresses made for her between March and May 1800 by Egan and Paul, Mantua Makers and three more, with belts, from Thomas Edward at 107, New Bond Street, though some of these dresses may have been for Frances. They were flimsy and chilly to wear, so Elizabeth had a velvet jacket and Frances a fine scarlet cloth spencer, which was a short, close-fitting jacket with a black velvet collar. For driving out, Elizabeth wore a 'fine green ladies cloth Phaeton Great coat' – suitably sturdy wear for open-top four-wheeled carriages drawn by a pair of horses.[107]

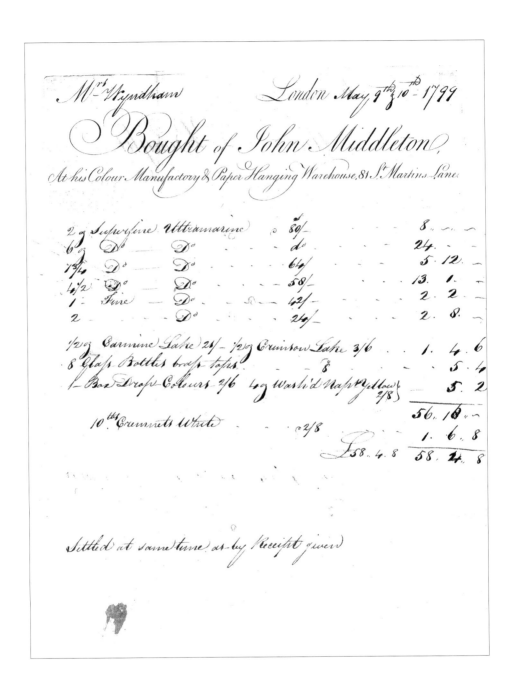

Bill from John Middleton, colour manufacturer 81, St. Martin's Lane, London, PHA 8064.

4. *Egremont's Countess*

Elizabeth's status at Petworth House towards the end of the 1790s was evidently enhanced. A new room was being made for her at the south of the House.[108] She could invite Farington to Petworth in the Earl of Egremont's name. In 1798, in one of his periodic new wills, the Earl appointed her, with William Long Kingsman, Doctor of Law, Lincoln's Inn Fields, as joint guardian of the children during their minorities with responsibility for the estates and properties bequeathed to them.[109]

At the beginning of July 1801 the Earl paid for 'a swing cott with an iron bowtop and mahogany standard frame; 9 yards of furniture dimity; 10 yards of fringe; an Irish cloth and wool mattress; and a white fustian and Down Pillow'.[110] On the 11th July he proposed a draft settlement on the intended marriage of George, 3rd Earl of Egremont, and Elizabeth Ilive[111] and on 16th July 1801 Elizabeth Ilive, spinster, married George O'Brien, Earl of Egremont, bachelor. They were married at Petworth by Thomas Vernon, the curate, and the witnesses were William Tyler, the lawyer and newly appointed steward of the Petworth estate, and John Upton.[112]

The marriage settlement stated that if Elizabeth survived the Earl, she was to receive an annuity of £2,000 during her lifetime, as her 'jointure in lieu of and in bar of her dower and thirds at Common Law and all claims thereto'. The annuity was to be raised as a rent charge on properties in several parishes in Sussex and was to be paid quarterly.[113]

The purchase of the 'cott' suggests an expected baby. Charles was five years old and since his birth there had apparently been no more babies – or

Petworth Park. Engraving by W. Westall, A.R.A., from a drawing by T. Henwood. By permission of West Sussex Record Office, WRSO PD 1072/1.

none that survived. If Elizabeth was sincere when she later told Humphry that she had not been desirous of being married, what made the Earl change his mind and encourage Elizabeth to do so? It may be that after fifteen years of their relationship he simply wanted to, but there may have been additional personal and economic reasons. The coming new baby due to be born after their marriage, would be the only legitimate child of their relationship and therefore heir to the Egremont estate and, if a boy, the title. The Earl of Egremont was fifty years old, not always in good health and had perhaps begun to think about the future of the estate and even more about the title. Would he rather it went to his heir than to his younger brothers or his nephew, none of whom he admired? The obituary of the Earl in the *Brighton Patriot* in November 1837 states that the Earl 'married the lady at a moment when he had reason to expect an increase in family'.[114] It would seem, however, that if Elizabeth was expecting a baby in the summer of 1801, it did not come to term. If nothing else, the marriage would give Elizabeth rights as his wife and protection after his death. At present she had none and was totally dependent on his good will.

Another suggested reason for the marriage comes in the correspondence referred to in chapter one, from the *Western Times* for July 1886.[115] A correspondent from Chelsea related a story told to her mother by her governess, a resident of Brighton. According to this story, Elizabeth 'was very desirous that the Earl should make her his wife, but when she pressed him to do so, he always replied evasively'. The story describes how Elizabeth 'feigned illness', persuaded a medical man to support her and the Earl was summoned to her death bed. She begged him to make an honest woman of her before she died, for her children's sake. The Earl eventually agreed and they were married privately by his chaplain. When the Earl discovered the trick, he refused to see her again. The writer suggested that the Earl's reluctance to marry her may have been because he had a wife still living and he could have been prosecuted for bigamy.

If this rather dramatic story has any truth in it, the Earl and Elizabeth must have been reconciled, as a last child was born to them, probably in February 1803. This baby, Lady Elizabeth Wyndham, has no known date of birth or official baptism, but an account of her birth and brief life has recently been discovered.[116] In 1847 Thomas Sockett, by then Rector of Petworth, must have been asking for information. In consequence, George Arnold of Petworth found in the Egremont Almshouse one Jane Lucas, who had been employed as a nursery maid, attendant to Lady Egremont and who was in the next room when the child was born. Jane Lucas remembered clearly that she saw the child when it was brought out of the bedroom to be dressed. She described it as 'a pretty baby, but turned very yellow'. From Jane Lucas' account it would seem that Lady Elizabeth's life was very brief. She stated that the infant was taken ill in the night and that, as no clergyman could be summoned in time, Lady Egremont's sister, 'Mrs. Meads', baptised the baby after its death.

Jane saw the baby again after it had died, and was one of those who carried the body to the church for burial. She also had to tell the Earl of the baby's death, at which 'he came out of his room and said 'why' and went into the room to see it'. Lady Elizabeth was buried by William Pullen, a local curate, in Petworth churchyard on 9th February 1803.[117] Even this caused problems: according to Jane Lucas, Mr. Vernon, the Petworth curate, refused to allow the burial as the child had not been officially baptised, until ordered to do so by the Bishop of Chichester, to whom the Earl had written on the subject.

Jane Lucas also reported that she heard Lady Egremont say:

... if the baby had lived, I should have been a happy woman, but now it is dead, I shall not be happy.

On 15th February, Ann Wild was paid £21 for acting as wet nurse 'to His Lordship's last (decd.)'.[118] This seems generous for a job that could not have lasted long. In March, Mary Berry submitted a bill for five weeks' attendance 'on Mrs. Wyndham on her lying in', so perhaps Elizabeth had a difficult childbirth.[119]

Not surprisingly, Elizabeth was ill at the beginning of 1803 and in March, Jane Lucas received extra payment of £1.1s. for 'setting up with Mrs. Wyndham'.[120] In March 1803 Elizabeth left Petworth and went up to the London house with her maid, Elizabeth Peacock, staying throughout April and May.[121] On 3rd May she was too ill to sign a proposed deed of separation, which was finally executed on 16th May 1803.[122]

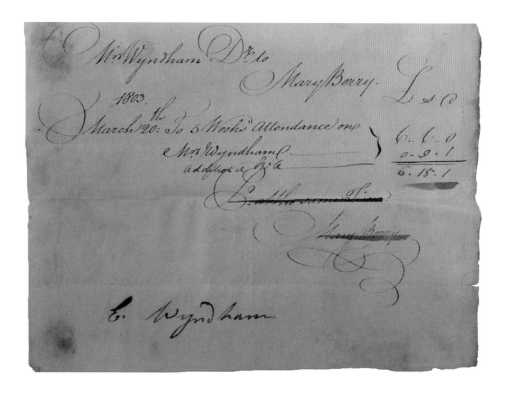

Bill submitted by Mary Berry, PHA 8025.

In June, Elizabeth took the landau she normally used when she was in London, two horses, two footmen, Birch and John Stedman, and drove away from Grosvenor Place never to return to live in either the Egremont London house or at Petworth again. Elizabeth Peacock quitted her service and took the coach back to Petworth.[123] The Countess's departure may have been sudden but maybe not unexpected, given the separation deed at the beginning of May. This was not purely a momentary flaring up of anger or disagreement. One of the few letters in which Elizabeth speaks for herself is one she wrote a month later to her daughter, Fanny, now fourteen years old:

Norwich July 14th, [1803]

My Dear Fanny,

We arrived at this place on the 11th. I am so very weak that I am not able to proseed without reasting for somedays. I have got the Coachman's Livery here for this town is almost as large as the City of London. Norwich is a very old Manufacturing town the Houses mostly built in the Raign of Elizabeth. Here is one of the largest Keeps I ever saw situated on a hill and is a most beautiful rising, the ditches which went round this keep (for there dose not appear there ever was a Castle) are all filled with Houses, so that the town is on the side of the Hill There is very little pavement all the Streets are pitched which makes it very disagreeable for foot passangers, my feet are so sore I can hardly put them to the ground. I have bought a shall [shawl] much cheaper than I could get it in London, and if you like it when I see you you shall have it. I have sent you and Charlotte a Jacobean pedgion from this place all the Weavers here bread them, and as I knew you ware fond of them. I hope your papa will not be angry at my sending

69

Norwich July 18.

My Dear Fanny

We arrived at this place on
the 11th I am so very weak. that I am not able
to proseed with out reasting for some days,
I have got the Coachmans Livery made for
this town is almost as large as the City of
London. Norwich is a very old Manufactering
town. the Houses movstly built in the Raign
of Elizabeth. here is one of the largest Keeps
I ever saw. situated on a hill and is a most
beautiful ring, the ditches which went round
thes Keep (for there dose not appear there ever
was a Castle) are all filled with Houses,
so that the town is on the side of the Hill
there is very little pavement all the Streets
are pitched which makes it very disagreeable
for foot passangers, my feet are so sore I can
hardly put them to the ground, I have bought
a shall, much cheaper than I could get it in
London, and if you like it when I see you you

have it. I have sent you and Charlotte a Jacobin
pigeon from this place all the weavers here
breed them, and as I knew you were fond of them
I hope your papa will not be angry at my
sending them. I leave this place tomorrow
or next day, but I hope to be able to hear
from you soon which will be as soon as
I settle for a little time, I hope you like
the jet Necklace I sent you of by the Coach
yesterday. Give my love to your papa and
your Sister and Brothers, and believe me
                my Dearest Fanny
            Your affectionate Mother
                    E. Wyndham

Letter from Elizabeth, written from Norwich, to her daughter Fanny, PHA 69.

them. I leave this place tomorrow or next day, but I hope to be able to hear from you soon which will be as soon as I settle for a little time, I hope you like the jet Necklace I sent you off by the coach yesterday. Give my love to your papa and your Sister and Brothers, and believe me

My Dearest Fanny,

your affectionate Mother,

E. Wyndham. [124]

Elizabeth's fashionable kid slippers that she had bought earlier at Hall's in Jermyn Street in London were not meant for sturdy walking on 'pitched' that is, cobbled, streets. The Norwich weavers were renowned for their wool, silk and cashmere shawls that were very expensive but increasingly fashionable accessories to insubstantial muslin dresses. In 1804 there were twelve manufacturers of shawls listed in the Norwich city directories. The weavers were also well-known for their Jacobin pigeons that flaunted a wide ruff of feathers around their necks.* The pigeons sent by Elizabeth arrived safely at Petworth. Robert Burfield charged 4s.8d. for carriage of a basket of pigeons by diligence on 19th July 1803.[125] 'Papa' would not be personally called upon to care for two pigeons, so the mention of his potential anger gives a possible indication of the emotion raised by the separation. Indeed, Percy Wyndham reportedly said that when Elizabeth left the Earl, his father George, then aged about sixteen, 'had been told to leave off writing' to his

---

* 'The Jacobin pigeon is distinguished by a remarkable ruff or frill of raised feathers, which commencing behind the head and proceding down the neck and breast, forms a kind of hood, not unlike that worn by a monk. Its flight is considerably impeded by the size and form of its hooded frill, and it keeps much at home and is well adapted for the aviary'. *The Book of Household Management*, Mrs. Isabella Beeton, 1880.

Blue, White and Black Jacobin Pigeons, engraver Vincent Brooks Day & Sons, *The Illustrated Book of Pigeons*. With standards for judging, Robert Fulton, Lewis Wright. Published by Cassell, Pelter & Galpin (1876?).

mother 'and having disobeyed was flogged by his father'.[126] However, in spite of Elizabeth feeling that the Earl might be angry, she still sends her love to 'your papa'. She gives no indication of why she is at Norwich, nor where she means to go – perhaps Fanny, who is now fourteen, already knows. Perhaps she was going to the property that the Earl owned in Norfolk.

By October, the separation of Elizabeth and the Earl was common knowledge. Elizabeth was now living in a house in Orchard Street in London. Humphry told Farington:

> The cause of their present unhappiness is Jealousy on her part. – She apprehends His Lordship is not faithful to her, – and that with people about her. – At present they do not cohabit.[127]

Elizabeth may have expected the Earl would change after their marriage and was disappointed. The death of Lady Elizabeth was tragic but the Earl may have hoped there would be more legitimate children as Elizabeth was only thirty-two. If she had stayed, there may well have been more children but she was ill, had had eight children, three of whom had died. She may well have not wanted any more pregnancies, especially if syphilis was a recurrent trauma or pregnancies and childbirth were increasingly difficult.

After Elizabeth's departure, life seems to have carried on without great disturbance at Petworth, although she did leave one noticeable gap. Farington noted that while Elizabeth 'resided there she sat at the top of the table'. Fanny, 'a pretty modest girl' now filled the gap left by her mother's departure by sitting on her father's right hand at the top of the dining-room table. 'She calls Lord E. Papa & He is very fond of Her'.[128]

However there was another departure from the household at this time. George like his mother, was also leaving home. The uneasy peace of Amiens had fallen apart and Great Britain was once again at war with France. George had been briefly in the navy but now, at sixteen, transferred into the 5th Dragoon Guards as a cornet – a junior officer – in the cavalry. Having granted power of attorney to his father he was drafted to join The *Monarch* at Deal at the end of November 1803. Tyler had the trying task of getting George to actually depart. On the 23rd November Tyler optimistically wrote to the Earl from London:

> [George] 'seems very desirous of deferring his departure till tomorrow when I think he will certainly go.'

And on November 26th:

> Mr. Wyndham very reluctantly left London yesterday morning at five o'clock by the Canterbury coach which he preferred to the Margate coach because The *Monarch* is lying nearer to the Downs than Margate and he intends to take a chaise from Canterbury to Deal. To this I could say nothing otherwise than that your Lordship's wishes were that he should go to Margate. I have paid him the £10 agreeably to your Lordship's directions.[129]

George may have resented being organised by Tyler, or it may be he had other fish to fry. His mother was now in London and Elizabeth may have felt acute dismay at seeing her first born going away to war. George sailed away suitably equipped with a regimental saddle and its accoutrements and bridle, leather breeches, regimental clothing, swords and a regimental trunk, the whole outfit cost £138.14*s*.[130]

Elizabeth's purchases at this time were of a quite different nature. As well as buying kid slippers, Elizabeth bought, from the haberdashers in London, a pair of fine, double cashmere garters and another pair in black cloth. These were made before the advent of elastic, but by 1803 there was a new fashion of inserting a spring inside garters to help them cling and hold up fine cotton hose. The haberdasher also supplied her with long grey and white kid gloves, several fine straw hats and ribbons. The new empire-line dresses called for a different shape of corset rather than stays. Elizabeth's were grey and acquired from Charles of Piccadilly, accompanied by six pairs of useful corded dimity pockets, to be worn around the waist under a dress or skirt.[131]

Her footmen, including Stedman and Birch, were splendid in blue cloth coats, black velveteen breeches, yellow cloth waistcoats with sleeves and hats trimmed with one-and-half-inch silver lace bands and cockades, the usual livery of the Egremont footmen.[132]

Bill from Thomas South silk mercer & laceman 'No 15, Leicester Square, Corner of the Panorama' London, PHA 7547.

5. *Egremont's Countess and William Blake*

The Caverns of the Grave Ive seen
And these I shewd to Englands Queen
But now the Caves of Hell I view
Who shall I Dare to shew them to
What mighty Soul in Beautys form
Shall dauntless View the Infernal Storm
Egremonts Countess can controll
The flames of Hell that round me roll
If she refuse I still go on
Till the Heavens & Earth are gone
Still admird by Noble minds
Followd by Envy on the winds
Reengravd Time after Time
Ever in their Youthful prime
My Designs unchangd remain
Time may rage but rage in vain
For above Times troubled Fountains
On the Great Atlantic Mountains
In my Golden House on high
There they Shine Eternally[133]

Whilst the trafficking in Great Masterpieces was taking place across the channel, William Blake and his wife Catherine – at the suggestion of John Flaxman the sculptor and at Hayley's instigation – left London and came down to live in a small cottage in Felpham on the Sussex coast.

Hayley was in distress in 1800 as Thomas Alphonso, his young son, had died in May. Blake, too, was beginning to 'emerge from a deep pit of melancholy'. An escape from London – and the prospect of an income from projected engravings to illustrate Hayley's forthcoming life of William Cowper – enhanced the prospect of this Sussex Eden. Blake visited Felpham in August 1800. Towards the end of September, he, Catherine and his sister, another Catherine, left Lambeth and journeyed down to Felpham.

Blake found the little cottage, set back a few minutes from the seashore, delightful, commenting that it was 'of cottages the prettiest'. He may never have seen the 'Atlantic mountains' before, but his wife and sister followed Hayley's regular practice and quickly took to the ocean's 'embrace'. Blake considered Felpham men to be 'the mildest of the human race'.[134]

Hayley was an enthusiastic, if overwhelming, patron. He kept Blake busy with his own and other commissions for engraving and miniatures. Nevertheless, there were excursions on foot and horseback to Hayley's old house at Eartham and to the house in Lavant, which was the home of Henrietta Poole, Hayley's great friend.[135] There is no known record of Blake having visited Petworth House, though of course he was in Petworth in October 1803, under rather different circumstances, when he made his first appearance before the court of Quarter Sessions on a charge of sedition.[136] Blake's impression of Elizabeth, given the eighteenth century's penchant for hyperbole, is powerful, a 'Mighty soul in Beauty's form' as he was later to describe her in his dedication of *Satan Calling up his Legions* inspired by Milton's *Paradise Lost*.

William Blake, *Satan Calling up his Legions*, tempera on canvas, 53.3 × 40.6 cm. Collins Baker No 427, courtesy of The National Trust.

By the time Blake began work on *Satan Calling up his Legions* in about 1804, when he had returned to London, Elizabeth had left the Egremont household and also settled in London. He was to paint several versions of *Satan Calling up his Legions*, dedicating the final version, in 1808, to 'a Lady of high rank', namely Elizabeth. The painting depicts the moment when Satan, cast down into hell by God, picked himself up out of the fiery pit crying 'Awake, arise, or be forever fallen'. In Blake's painting, Satan

> ...above the rest
> In shape and gesture proudly eminent
> Stood like a tower...[137]

Whilst Blake was working on the different versions of *Satan Calling up his Legions* he encountered a painful rejection of his work and a painful cancellation of his prospective income in his disagreement with the publisher Robert H. Cromek. In 1805 Cromek commissioned him to illustrate a prospective elegant edition of Robert Blair's popular 'gothick' poem *The Grave*, originally published in 1743. This new edition was to be dedicated to Queen Charlotte and had an impressive list of sponsors. Blake produced twenty designs for one guinea each and expected to have more money for executing the engravings for publication himself. To his acute disappointment and chagrin, Cromek instead hired a fashionable engraver, Louis Schiavonetti, who received £600 to produce twelve final engravings selected from Blake's original designs.

One of Blake's designs for *The Grave* had been the *Day of Judgement*; based on the age-old doom theme of Christ in Glory, with the souls of the saved rising to heaven on his right hand and the damned falling to hell on his left. His stalwart patron, Thomas Butts, in 1806, as balm to Blake's anger and injured pride, commissioned Blake to paint a watercolour version of the *Day of Judgement* for him. This painting Blake called *A Vision of the Last Judgement*. Humphry the next year asked Elizabeth to commission another version; Elizabeth could thus add the value of her patronage and, above all, money. Executed in pencil, ink and watercolour on paper, with yet more figures added, the picture was finished in February 1808. Blake wrote Humphry a detailed description of his work:

> The design of *The Last Judgement*, which I have completed by your recommendation for the Countess of Egremont, it is necessary to give some account of; and its various parts ought to be described, for the accommodation of those who give it the honour of their attention.[138]

The Last Judgement was one of two pictures shown by Blake at the Royal Academy Exhibition in 1808. There is no record of what Elizabeth paid Blake when she commissioned her version. Did Elizabeth go to see her picture at the Royal Academy and did she visit the exhibition Blake later organised in his brother's house in Broad Street in 1809 that included another version of *Satan Calling Up His Legions*? By this time she was living in Hurlingham House, on the banks of the Thames in Fulham. Did the two pictures hang in that house, before they were finally absorbed before 1835 into the Earl's collection at Petworth where they can still be seen today?

William Blake, *The Last Judgement*, pen and ink, pencil and watercolour, 50.8 × 39.4 cm. Collins Baker No 454, courtesy of The National Trust.

6. *A New Life in London*

If Elizabeth had a separation settlement of £2,000 a year, similar to that cited in the Earl's will which was made on their marriage,[139] she was a wealthy and socially acceptable Countess of Egremont, well able to afford to sponsor Blake's picture.

Elizabeth may have gone seldom to London before her marriage but, after she left the Earl of Egremont in 1803, she settled in Orchard Street one of the most fashionable areas of the West End.[140] Orchard Street, built in the middle of the eighteenth century, runs between Oxford Street and Portman Square. Elizabeth was less than a mile from the Egremont town house in Grosvenor Place. Her brother Thomas, an apothecary, lived with his wife and family in rather less aristocratic surroundings off Russell Square and there were friends, such as Humphry, who had visited at Petworth but lived in London. According to title deeds, Elizabeth also lived at White House, Sudbury, Harrow after September 1803 until about November 1805.[141] This was possibly an additional country residence while she was living in Orchard Street.

She was to live twenty years in London but we have only sporadic glimpses of her life there. Detailed records of her activities were not stored in the Petworth House Archives as she was no longer a member of the Egremont household. Her grandson, Percy Wyndham, gives vague and sometimes erroneous details of his grandmother's life but does say that by 1807, when Elizabeth was living in Fulham, her house 'was much frequented by scientific people'.[142] We might like to think this was, indeed, true but there is no apparent evidence to confirm it was so.

We do not know how much she saw of the Earl and whether they visited each other, but sporadic rumour that they were to live together again and occasional references in the Petworth House Archives to the Earl being at Fulham, suggest they did. Indeed, the house he eventually bought there for his estranged countess was grand enough to suit an earl. She certainly remained a strong presence in her children's lives. Whilst they were still young they continued under the supervision of Thomas Sockett, the tutor to Henry and Charles, with a governess for Frances and Charlotte. When Elizabeth left, her eldest child, George, was sixteen, but her youngest, Charles, was only seven. All three sons went into the Army. Frances, her eldest daughter, seems to have been especially close to her mother, as Elizabeth's letter to her from Norwich suggests. There remains a strong tie throughout the next twenty years. Her mother was present and signed as a witness at Frances' wedding to Charles Merrik Burrell, on 8th August 1808, at the fashionable St. George's, Hanover Square.[143] Charles and Frances Burrell thereafter figure in accounts of family gatherings in London and Sussex. In more homely fashion, sausages were still being sent from Elizabeth's London household to the Burrell family at Knepp Castle, in Sussex, until a few months before Elizabeth died.[144]

George Wyndham, safely home from the Napoleonic wars when they ended in 1815, married Mary Blunt,* a local girl from Crabbet Park near Horsham, Sussex. As soon as Mary accepted his proposal, she went to

* Mary Blunt, the daughter of the reverend William Blunt and Mary Glanville. Wilfred Scawen Blunt was Mary's nephew.

85

we give five guineas per week. In a few days
we shall remove in to No 9 Nelsons Crescent
a most elegant house & pay no more than
one pound ten shillings per week. I went
in sea to day for the first time it was very
warm & I liked it much & intend if it agrees
with me to bath all next month & if it is fine
you often wish you & your sister with us Pray
give my love to her & best comp.ts to your Father
likewise Mr. Cockburn & believe My Dear Miss Shirley

Yours truly & sincerely

P.S.
Elizabeth Egremont

Pray has Smithers paid the money

Oct. 26th Prospect Row
Ramsgate

11

D3794/13/1A

Part of letter written from Prospect Row, Ramsgate by Elizabeth to her friend
Miss Frances Shirley, 26 October 1815. Courtesy of Staffordshire Record Office
D3794/13/1A.

London with her mama and straight-way was taken to see and be seen by George's mother the Countess of Egremont, Frances and Charles Burrell and the younger Wyndham children. In the summer of 1818 Elizabeth spent some months staying with the family at their country houses in Sussex: with George and Mary at 'Drove' and with Henry and his wife Elizabeth at 'Sladeland'.[145]

Other activities are occasionally mentioned in the society columns of contemporary newspapers and other sources. In October 1815 Elizabeth wrote to a friend, Miss Frances Shirley of Park Street, Grosvenor Square, giving an account of her visit to the Kent seaside and her first bathe in the sea. Elizabeth found the countryside from London to Dover 'very pleasant, but, extremely hilly'. She was sorry that she had not been better informed about Dover which proved to be 'very dirty nothing but Stenches is to be smelt in their houses & in the Town nothing but Sailors'. Elizabeth goes on to say:

> You may be sure we did not stay long in this disagreeable place but sent the servant to Ramsgate who procured for us a house at No 7 Prospect Row it is very comfortable on account of the Parlours answering for a Drawing Room we give five guineas per week. In a few days we shall remove in to No 19 Nelsons Crescent a most elegant house & pay no more than one pound ten shillings per week. I went in Sea to day for the first time it was very warm & I liked it much & in tend if it agrees with me to Bath all next month if it is fine.

Elizabeth was certainly made of stern stuff if she planned to continue bathing in the sea into November. Not surprisingly, her friend replied, 'I fear you will not be able to continue the cold Bathe so late in the year.'[146]

In April 1817 the 'Countess of Egremont's ball' was held in Dover Street, Mayfair. This was a quadrille party 'given to a juvenile circle' who

> assembled at ten o'clock and broke up at two. Refreshments were provided, consisting of every delicacy. The company were highly delighted – of course they did not separate without regret [147]

Nelson Crescent & Prospect Row, Ramsgate, courtesy of Phil Spain, http://ramsgatehistory.com.

In October of that year, Elizabeth set off from Cook's Hotel, Albemarle Street on a tour.[148] Two years later, in August 1819, she went to Paris.[149]

The Earl and Elizabeth may have stayed on amicable terms. The Earl was responsible for providing her with a home, renting 'quite a small house' in Montagu Square in 1805, 'only two rooms on each floor, three in basement and attic' at an annual rent of £157.10s.[150] Later, in 1807, he bought Hurlingham House in Fulham, for £16,000 plus £2,000 for furniture and fittings,[151] to be Elizabeth's for her lifetime. Nevertheless, there had been conflict, at least during the first years of separation. In 1804 the Earl would not pay the tax due on the landau in which Elizabeth had driven away the previous year.[152] 1805 seems to have been a fraught year: 'I am sorry Lord and Lady Egremont's disagreement has terminated so seriously' wrote Susanna Thomas to Ozias Humphry.[153]

In 1807 Elizabeth moved from fashionable Mayfair to elegant Hurlingham House on the north bank of the Thames in still largely rural Fulham, an area supporting many market gardens and suitably secluded mental asylums. Nevertheless, London was beginning to spread out its tentacles of bricks and mortar with more and more houses and streets being built in Fulham. The move for Elizabeth from a relatively small town house in London to Hurlingham was significant.

Hurlingham House, originally built in 1760, had been greatly enlarged in 1797 and stood in twenty acres of land. When the Earl of Egremont bought the estate from John Ellis in 1807, the house contained many bedrooms, dressing rooms, boudoirs, large and small dining rooms, servants' quarters for housemaids, a butler, and the housekeeper. At the top of the house there were extensive attics. Outside, there was a dairy, wood house, laundry, stables, coachman's quarters, gardeners' apartments, an orchard, walled garden, kitchen garden, hothouse and ice-house.[154] It may be that Elizabeth

Hurlingham by Fulham, Seat of John Ellis Esqr July 1799, courtesy of the Hurlingham Club.

did entertain scientists and men and women of note; she had room. She certainly had acres of land for any agricultural projects she wished to pursue and gardens for her own planning. The Reverend Wood, vicar of Fulham, said she used to sell the fruit alone from the estate for £50 a year. The vicar also said he was under great obligations to Lady Egremont for seconding him in his plans for the improvement of the parish, though there is apparently no record of what these plans were.[155]

Her brother, Thomas Hamilton Ayliffe, and his family seem to have been well in evidence and were probably physically so at Hurlingham House.[156] Joseph Jinks, brother of Thomas' wife Hester, was to remark that Elizabeth advanced considerable sums towards the maintenance of her brother and family – the Earl of Egremont directly or indirectly did so, too.[157] In July 1817, Jinks told the Earl that Lady Egremont had intended to build ten houses for her brother and ten for each sister. However, Thomas was unable to keep the ten that he had had built, when the Earl insisted that his loan of £500 be repaid.

Thomas, through ineptitude or ill-fortune, was constantly in need of money. The apothecary's shop in Bernard Street did not flourish and Thomas seems to have indulged in ill-starred property speculation, from which he evidently hoped the Earl, on Elizabeth's urging, would rescue him.[158] His family seem to have clung to Elizabeth for financial support and were living with her at the time of her death. Doubtless, she provided money on occasion – and the Earl paid for suits of clothes for the boys.[159]

In 1815, Elizabeth left Hurlingham House, which was let to the Archbishop of Dublin* for two years – she was to receive the income from the rent for herself. She let 'a small piece of ground and orchard' to Joseph

---

* Euseby Cleaver, was at one time tutor to the Earl of Egremont, and had the livings of Tillington and Petworth.

Smithers for one hundred guineas per annum, twenty-five guineas per quarter,[160] apparently having difficulty in getting the money out of him, for her friend Miss Shirley wrote

> We went to Mr. Benbow the other day to enquire if Smithers had paid his rent but found he had not. Mr. B told us he was coming to Baker Street to see you about it to know if he might make use of Lord Egremonts name to enforce payment . . . [161]

Elizabeth hoped that she might be able to sue for the rent owing.[162]

In the next few years, she lived in various rented properties in and around London, including Baker Street.[163] In January 1819 she left 'her seat in Putney' and arrived 'at her new residence in Waterloo-place' – a very prestigious address.[164] This implies that she had been occupying another property south of the river Thames in Putney, to which no other reference has yet been found.

Despite this fashionable residence in Waterloo Place, Elizabeth kept quite a small establishment in her final year. Her butler, Mark Delloca, came from Paris; besides him she also had a footman and two female staff who lived in and a coachman. A charwoman and a laundress came in as required.[165] It seems that, like most ladies of the day Elizabeth spent part of her time reading or doing embroidery and tapestry. In March 1822 the Countess bought Walter Scott's latest novel *The Fortunes of Nigel* and William Combe's *Dr. Syntax in Paris* which had been published in 1820. Joseph Graham sent Elizabeth a bill for a footstool he had upholstered with 'your needlework cover'.[166] She spent £10.15*s* on boots and shoes for her niece, Fanny Courtney*, one of Thomas Ayliffe's daughters and, in June, ordered a 'super fine blue coat' for her at a cost of £4.10*s*.[167]

Waterloo Place and Part of Regent Street drawn by Thomas Hosmer Shepherd, engraved by W. Tombleson. From *London in the Nineteenth Century*, T. H. Shepherd, published by James Elmes in 1828.

* Frances Ayliffe had married Francis de Courtney.

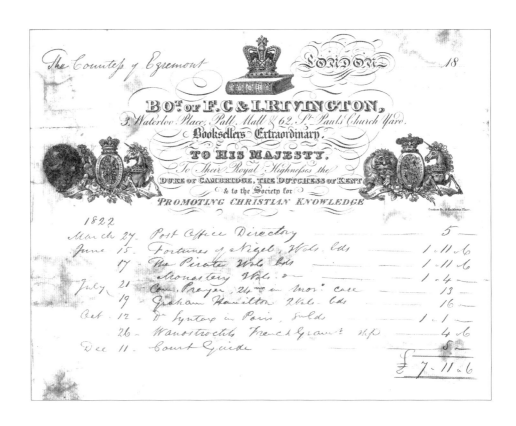

Bill from F. C & I. Rivington, Booksellers Extraordinary, '3 Waterloo Place, Pall Mall & 62 St. Paul's Church Yard', London, PHA 7547.

7. The Death of the Countess

Elizabeth appears to have been seriously ill from the middle of November 1822. She had a nurse from 14th November who was paid £1.1s a week and supplied with a gown and bonnet costing £1.6s 6d.[168] There were regular bills for medicine, including castor oil, cascara, cochine and unspecified powders from mid-November onwards. In December there were bills for jellies, Florence wine – a red wine from Tuscany – syrup of rhubarb, elderflower and rose water. Mr. Pettigrew, the surgeon, submitted an account of £10 for attending to Elizabeth and to Mrs. Courtney, who was living in Elizabeth's house 'in her confinement'.* By 19th December, Elizabeth's condition had deteriorated: leeches were applied and these were followed by a large 'blister' or caustic poultice.[169]

All was to no avail, for, on 31st December, the Earl of Egremont received an express from London saying that Lady Egremont had died suddenly the previous night.[170] On the first day of the New Year the Earl, Charlotte Wyndham, Henry Wyndham, his wife and George Wyndham with his wife went to London. The next day, Mary, Elizabeth's daughter-in-law, visited Waterloo Place with Charlotte, who left town on the 4th January with her father, presumably for Petworth. On the 8th January, George and Henry, Elizabeth's eldest sons, left London for Orchard Wyndham,* their estate in Williton, Somerset to attend 'poor Lady Egremont's funeral'.[171]

* A daughter was born to 'the Lady of Frances de Courtnay' on 29 December 1822. The birth at Waterloo Place, was announced in *The Morning Post* on 31 December 1822.
* Orchard Wyndham was the family seat of the Wyndhams before they inherited Petworth.

The seventy year old Earl did not travel with them, perhaps because he was often in bad health in the winter.

It is open to question why Elizabeth was buried in the ancient Wyndham family vault in St. Decuman's church at nearby Watchet.[172] Maybe, since Elizabeth had left him, the Earl wanted to avoid the embarrassment of her burial at Petworth but wished to accord her the status due to her position as Countess of Egremont by choosing, instead, the Wyndham vault. It was a long haul down to Somerset in the dark days of midwinter and the journey of over one hundred and twenty miles took several days over bad roads. George Wyndham was eventually to quibble over the expense in the account rendered by the undertakers. Local women, Jenny Stevens and Mary Lee, had to open up, air and prepare the family house at Orchard Wyndham for George and Henry's reception and clean up after they departed. They were paid for two weeks work. Colonel Meade – Elizabeth's brother-in-law – and Thomas Ayliffe stayed in nearby Watchet.

The funeral was organised by Thomas but all the bills were paid by the Earl. As well as the disputed undertaker's bill these included comprehensive mourning wardrobes for all the Ayliffe family, Colonel and Mrs. Meade, the Courtneys and the servants at Waterloo Place. The local Somerset tailors were kept busy making black jackets; waistcoats; breeches; hat bands and gloves for the pall bearers, mutes, tenant farmers and numerous labourers who looked after the horses and escorted the coffin to the funeral at St. Decuman's. The labourers were also paid 2s.6d a head for attending and assisting at the funeral and twelve torch carriers were on call 'if wanted'.

The cortege was headed by 'Mr. Williams, the undertaker, mounted, with Satin Scarf and Hat Band'; he was followed by . . .

'Two Mutes mounted – Twenty of my Lord's Tenants mounted, with

Orchard Wyndham, the Seat of the Earl of Egremont 1839 by John Buckler, Pigott
Collection 6.251 Court. Inst. negative 762/31 (25a), by permission of the Somerset
Archaeological and Natural History Society.

Cloaks and Sarsnet Hat Bands two and two – Eight under Bearers mounted, all in new Black Clothes ditto – Two Horse porters – Two Clergymen in a private Chariot – State Horse with the Coronet & Cushions, the bearer uncovered – The Hearse drawn by b[lack] Horses – Two Chief Mourners, (the Col. Wyndhams') sons of dec'ed. – Two other Mourners (Mr. Aileff & Col. Meade, brother & brother in law of the dec'ed) – Two Domestics of deceased – Eight pall Bearers – Mr. Tripp's and Mr. Leigh's private Carriages.'[173]

Within St. Decuman's Church, masons and carpenters had opened up the vault, which was then hung with black cloth and the blacksmith was paid to make 'iron bars used about the vault'. The stone bearing Elizabeth's coat of arms was to be inscribed:

THE RIGHT HON ^{BLE}

ELIZABETH,

Countess of Egremont

Died 30 th *Dec:* ^{r}

1822.

Aged 53 Years.

The validity of the Ayliffe coat of arms is questionable. Thomas seems to have put it together in the months before Elizabeth died with the help of William Radclyffe, considered by contemporary opinion as a somewhat dubious member of the College of Heralds, who charged £262. 17s. 2d.

Opposite. Design for proposed memorial to Elizabeth Countess of Egremont. DD\WY/199, by permission of South West Heritage Trust. The design is held at the Somerset Heritage Centre.

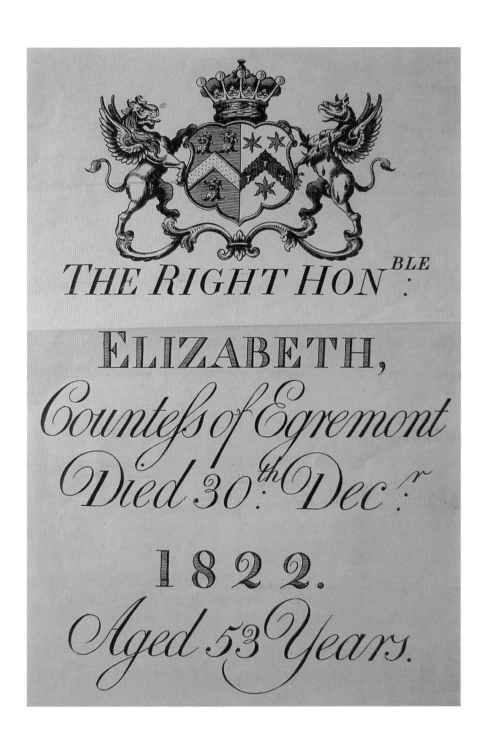

THE RIGHT HON.^{BLE}:

ELIZABETH,

Countess of Egremont

Died 30th: Dec.^r

1822.

Aged 53 Years.

for his work. It is not known whether Elizabeth herself had agreed to this expense. There is no visible sign of any memorial to Elizabeth outside the vault today.

After the interment there was beef and ale for the farmers and others at the 'New Inn' and the 'Coach and Horses' at nearby Williton. In London, the Waterloo Place servants were given notice. The Earl of Egremont paid various accounts after Elizabeth's death, including £529 for Messrs. Simpson and Giblet, the undertakers; £252. 6s. 2d. to Thomas Ayliffe for the expenses of the funeral.[174] The servants were discharged in February, being paid their wages and only a small gratuity, since none of them had been with Elizabeth for more than three years. William Tyler, the Earl's agent, hoped that the lease of the house could be surrendered on Lady Day.[175] Tyler, who many found very objectionable, seems to have had tender memories of Elizabeth, daring to ask the Earl for some little memento of her, in memory of better and happier days.[176]

Immediately after Elizabeth's death, Thomas sent all her outstanding bills to William Tyler. Tyler paid some major bills, such as the coach-maker's bill for £605. 4s. 8d., directly, but Thomas must have offered to act as his agent to pay the smaller bills. Tyler was very grateful for this, as he was very busy at the time and he told the Earl that 'Mr. Ayliffe's payment of the bills will relieve me of some loss of time here.'[177]

In June 1823, Thomas claimed to have paid the bills, but that he had left the bills and the receipts with Mr. Gadd of Pall Mall Arcade. However, since Mr. Gadd was now in France, Thomas could not get at them. It would seem, from the receipts, that Thomas did not actually pay the bills until October 1823, although he had been given £850 for their payment in February 1823 and a further £40 in June.[178] Finally, in November, Thomas was paid £24. 3s. 9d. as the balance of the amount he had paid out for bills and taxes:[179] and he signed a receipt on the 10th November for a total of £914. 3s. 9d:

on account of debts and taxes owing by the late Countess of Egremont and which have been discharged by me according to account delivered [180]

The business of Thomas' payment of the bills did not quite end in November 1823. In March 1824, the Earl received a letter from Howell and James the haberdashers and mercers who had, among other things, supplied mourning for Thomas and his family. Thomas had given them a draft for £60 in part payment of the money owing on their bills, but it had been returned dishonoured. Since they had learnt that Thomas was in the King's Bench, or Rules, debtors' prison, they hoped that the Earl would pay their outstanding bills.[181]

It is perhaps significant that in September 1823 Thomas Ayliffe took out

Bill from Howell & James, Furriers & Lace Merchants, Silk Mercers, Drapers & Haberdashers, 9, Regent Street, Pall Mall, Removed from 89, Pall Mall late Dyde & Scribe, PHA 7547.

a policy with Sun Fire Insurance for £1,000 for his brick dwelling house, 18 New Ormond Street, and the fixtures therein, to cover 'Household Goods Wearing apparel printed books & plate, Musical instruments, Pictures & prints frames & Glass included, China & Glass',[182] suggesting that he had acquired some of these desirable goods after the death of his sister. In February 1824, some table and bed linen with the Egremont coronet and initial on them were being offered for sale as an unredeemed pawnbroker's pledge and had to be bought back by the Earl's London house steward. They had been pledged by Mrs. Thomas H. Ayliffe for her husband's debt, after the death of the

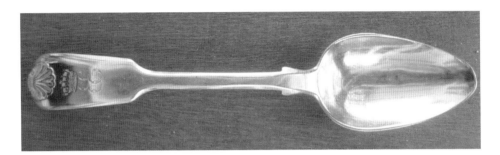

Countess.[183] Evidently, Thomas managed to keep at least some of Elizabeth's possessions as a souvenir, for some monogrammed silver spoons and forks have survived in the ownership of a family of descendants in Australia and are much treasured. Two spoons bear the Wyndham crest and another, the coronet of the Countess with her initials EE – Elizabeth Egremont.[184] Unsurprisingly, later in 1824 Thomas Ayliffe, as Howell and James had discovered, was in the King's Bench prison for debt.[185] In 1825 he appeared as a surgeon in a list of insolvent debtors, with his last address given as Compton near Plymouth, Devon.[186] He was still in Devon in 1830 when he wrote to his daughter, Fanny Courtney, now living in Paris. The family seemed to be in distress: 'Ever since I have been in the country I have not been able to pay my bills'[187] and he deplored the fact he could never afford to send his sons to school. 'I have Three sons and do not know what to do with them' he wrote to the Earl in 1831.[188] Nevertheless, he had a yacht *Britannia* that cost £215 and he hoped to sell her for at least one hundred and sixty guineas. The Wyndhams were 'all too distant and haughty' – could Thomas or his family expect anything from the Earl of Egremont's will?[189] They could not: but after the Earl died in 1837, his son George Wyndham, did do something for them. He paid for their passage to Australia, which ultimately proved to be beneficial for the Ayliffe family.

In 1839, George, Henry and Charles acquired a Royal Licence to use the surname of Wyndham instead of Wyndham Ilive[190] – and so Elizabeth was expunged from their lives and any public records from then on. Within two generations, no-one in the family seems to have known anything about her origins – hence all the speculation. Did her own children never know, or

Opposite. Silver spoon bearing the Countess's initials and coronet. Private collection, photographs provided by Anne Monk.

was it George Wyndham who discouraged any enquiry about it? Like many people of his day, he could not come to terms with his illegitimacy. In *Burke's Peerage*,[191] printed in the mid-nineteenth century, George Wyndham, by then Lord Leconfield, is described as the adopted son of the 3rd Earl of Egremont – there is no mention of a mother. The family must have agreed that information. By the time that Hugh Wyndham was writing his *Family History* in 1950,[192] he was, of course, describing the past, which made it possible to name Elizabeth without being controversial.

Elizabeth, Countess of Egremont, certainly had a life of startling contrasts: from the family of an impoverished printer, her mother in a London workhouse, to life in a huge country mansion, with artists and men of science visiting its hospitable host and a regiment of servants to wait on her and her growing family of children. Even after her separation from the Earl, Elizabeth continued to enjoy a large house, servants, the company of men of science and patronage of artists. It was not unknown at this period for aristocrats to marry women from a level of society far beneath them but, in most of these cases, the women were known to have been courtesans, actresses or singers. Nothing like this has ever been said about Elizabeth and, surely, had there been any whisper of the sort, it would have been picked up by one of the contemporary diarists or gossip writers. She would seem to have been respectable in everything except her connection with the Earl.

Elizabeth must have had extraordinary qualities to have attracted the Earl and been installed as his principal mistress, with their children his acknowledged family. She was intelligent enough to conduct and write up scientific experiments – where and when she had received a scientific education is unclear. Her father's family was obviously educated but not necessarily in science and Elizabeth was only about seven when he died in straitened circumstances. She is not mentioned as being in the workhouse with her mother in 1778: had Elizabeth perhaps been taken in by a relative, who could offer her a means of education? Or did the Earl organise her education, since she was so young when they met. There are still so many unanswered questions.

What is certain is that Elizabeth's connection with the Earl gave her the chance to exercise the intelligence and pursue the interests that she had. It gave her a life of wealth and comfort, a chance to travel and children and grandchildren to visit. Emotionally, her life may have been hard, even before her separation from the Earl. How did Elizabeth feel when she was installed at Petworth; what was the attitude of the servants to her? Her sons' tutor, Thomas Sockett, was the nearest to her in social origin but she was elevated by the Earl's choice of her: firstly as his mistress and, subsequently, as his wife. Therefore, it is understandable that she found his unfaithfulness – 'and that with people about her' – difficult to accept.

For whatever reason, the marriage lasted only two years before Elizabeth left the Earl but their relationship was strong enough for something to survive the separation. However, that relationship remained contradictory: she sent love to 'Papa' when writing to their daughter Frances; there are constant hints in the documents of the Earl being regularly at Hurlingham; yet their grandson, Percy Wyndham, stated that his father had been 'thrashed' for keeping in touch with Elizabeth against the Earl's wishes.

Although Elizabeth was apparently brushed out of the family history, it was her eldest son by the Earl, George Wyndham, who inherited Petworth and the other un-entailed estates from his father. The Orchard Wyndham estate in Somerset and the title went to the Earl's nephew, but it is Elizabeth's descendants who still live at Petworth House, where she spent so many years of her intriguing life.

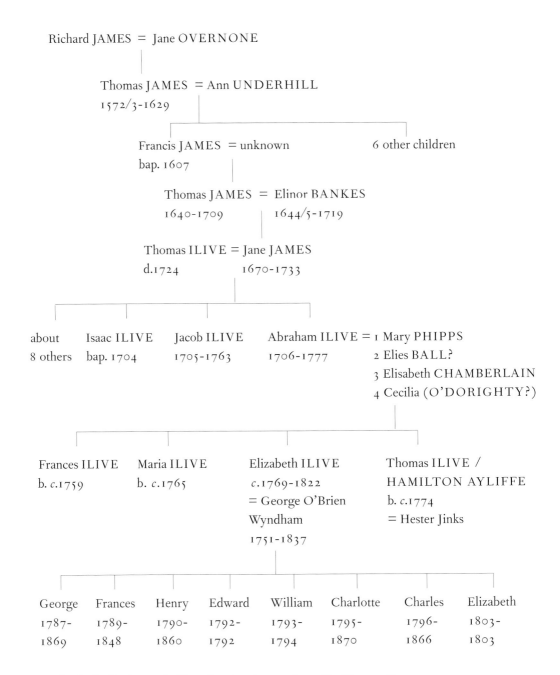

Elizabeth Ilive's Family Tree showing descent from Dr. Thomas James.

Elizabeth Ilive has always been a shadowy figure and we are not the first to be curious about the differing suggestions of her background which have appeared in various publications over the years.

Stories originate from Australia where Elizabeth's brother, Thomas Hamilton Ayliffe, emigrated after the death of the Earl. Thomas and, later, his grand-daughter, Cecilia Wyndham Hill, told exciting tales of romance and derring-do. He said that he remembered his father's night-time escape, wearing a glittering uniform, plumed hat and bejewelled sword and how, after his departure, their beautiful, weeping mother was forced to live in anonymity in a hidden cottage instead of their castle. She was no longer to be called 'My Lady' but 'Mrs. Ilive'. Given that earlier Ilives are now known to have been Jacobite supporters, perhaps similar stories were handed down through the generations and by the time they reached Thomas, he believed them to have involved his own family.

Thomas said that he and his sisters were sent by boat to Germany and on to France accompanied by a priest and servants, where the girls were placed in a convent for their education – and, certainly, Elizabeth must have received a reasonably good education somewhere. However, it now seems possible that she may have spent at least part of her early childhood with her mother in a London workhouse – hardly something to be acknowledged in her now elevated circumstances. Perhaps we will never know where Elizabeth was educated, but we have had a fascinating time attempting to solve the mystery of her background.

When Sheila Haines and I first started work to establish Elizabeth's true identity there were several leads and theories of our own to explore as well as the very intriguing tales that were promoted by Thomas and his grand-daughter in Australia. We tried to follow up the contemporary opinion that Elizabeth was a farmer's daughter, possibly from the West Country. We did not find any likely records at the Somerset Record Office and a list of tenant farmers from the Wyndham estates in Somerset, held in the Petworth House Archives, did not yield any clues, either.

We wondered if Elizabeth was an actress – given that the Earl liked to go to the theatre and one of his other mistresses, Eliza Fox, was on the stage. Eliza's father, Joseph Fox, ran the theatre in Brighton where the Earl had a house. Searching through Brighton newspapers of the time, we discovered a Mr. and Mrs. Iliff appearing on stage in the town at the right date. Further research at the British Library gave us the names of actors Mr. Edward Henry Iliff and his wife Mrs. Maria Iliff, née Palmer.[193] We had not found Elizabeth, although this couple were very interesting in themselves.

Some nineteenth century sources suggest that her father was the Reverend Iliff, a master at Westminster School. However, Westminster school was unable to provide any record of the Reverend Iliff having been a master there. A theory that George O'Brien Wyndham may have been taught by the Reverend Iliffe at Westminster and met Elizabeth while he was a schoolboy there is impossible since she was twenty years his junior and was not even born when he attended the school. As other researchers have pointed out, there was a Reverend Thomas Iliff of Dean's Yard, Westminster, who died in 1803. His will, proved on 30th September 1803, is available from The National Archives.[194] The Reverend Iliff came from a Leicestershire family and became the librarian at Westminster Cathedral. Reverend Iliff names several children in his will, two of whom do indeed, correspond with the names of Elizabeth's siblings Frances and Thomas – but no mention is made of a daughter named Elizabeth. It has been suggested that this is because she was already married to the Earl at the time the will was made and her father would have no need to leave her a bequest. At the City of Westminster Archives I looked at an original parish register of St. Clement Danes, London and confirmed the baptisms of several children of Reverend Thomas Iliff and his wife Frances, including Elizabeth Iliff, baptised on 14 September 1776. Nothing indicates that she was more than a few months old at the time, which would mean that this Elizabeth would only have been aged about eleven in 1787 when George, the son of Elizabeth and the Earl of Egremont, was born. We assume that the Reverend Iliff's daughter may have died at some time before the will was made but it has not been practical to find a burial in London with no exact date or place to go on and we could not find her name in any indexes.

William Tiffin Iliff, a nephew of Reverend Iliff, transcribed and annotated *The Monumental Inscriptions of St. Mary, Newington, Surrey* which was privately printed in 1880. In this, he refers to the Reverend Iliff's son, Thomas Iliff, recording that he was a major in the East India Company and had died on the Isle of Wight. Unfortunately, we have been unable to find a reference to him in either the East India Company records or in the burial indexes of the Isle of Wight Record Office to confirm this. Coincidentally, one of the sons of the Reverend Thomas Iliff, named in his will, was the aforementioned actor, Edward Henry Iliff, who took administration of the will.

Percy Wyndham, son of Elizabeth's son George, thought that Elizabeth's father was possibly the Vicar of Bramley in Surrey. However, a search of the Bramley parish registers and the name indexes at the Surrey History

Centre revealed no evidence that a Reverend Ilive was ever the incumbent of that parish or other Surrey parishes.

In 2014, we were presented with yet another theory as to Elizabeth's parentage. A family in Uruguay who are descended from Lord Robert Clive of India have a long-standing, oral tradition that Elizabeth Ilive was actually his daughter, Elizabeth Clive, baptised in Shropshire in 1764.[195] This put an intriguing and totally new slant on the matter and one for which we have no explanation.

We considered the possibility – as did others – that Elizabeth and her siblings may have been baptised in the Catholic Church and that this would account for the lack of records to be found in Church of England parish records. Jeremy Masters, a descendant of Thomas Hamilton Ayliffe, who has now done extensive work on the history of the Ilive family, found that eight children of Thomas and Hester Ilive were baptised in Catholic chapels in London. He also found that the apothecary John Gabb, to whom Thomas had been apprenticed, was Catholic.[196] However, no such records have yet been found regarding Elizabeth.

When Thomas Hamilton Ayliffe arrived in Australia he was in a position, as so many others did, to reinvent himself. Much information about his supposed family background has been available online for some years and some of it is, indeed, accurate. Certainly, the names of his father and mother, Abraham and Cecilia Ilive, are proven now. However, a marriage record for them has yet to be discovered so we still cannot confirm that Cecilia's maiden name was O'Dorighty, as her Australian descendants believe – though there is no reason to doubt this. It seems increasingly likely that some areas of the story are based on fact but, over the years, other parts must have been exaggerated or made up entirely. It is not at all uncommon for family stories to change in this way as they are passed down the generations.

We realised that one way to try and confirm the father of the Ilive children was through Thomas's apprenticeship records. Apprenticeship records from the Society of Apothecaries in London reveal that the father of Thomas Ilive was, indeed, called Abraham and that he died in Oxford in 1777.[197] This is backed up in a contemporary report of 1778, by the author E. Rowe Moores, who also states that Abraham died in Oxford in 1777.[198]

Right at the start of our research, we were aware of an Abraham Ilive, son of Thomas and Jane Ilive, living in Aldersgate, London. However, this Abraham was baptised in 1706 and, therefore, seemed rather old to be a suitable candidate for the father of Elizabeth, born in 1770. Having searched parish records and contemporary newspapers at the Oxfordshire Record Office and discovered the newspaper petition addressed to members of the University of Oxford described in Chapter One, we are now convinced that, despite his advanced years, this was indeed her father.

Oxford features greatly in the Ilive family background. According to the aforementioned petition, Abraham's 'great grandfather' – actually his great-great grandfather – was Dr. Thomas James, appointed in 1602 as librarian of the Bodleian Library in Oxford. Thomas James, son of Richard James and Jane Overnone, was born on the Isle of Wight in 1572/3 and studied at New College, Oxford. He became rector of St. Aldate's, Oxford in 1602 and a month later married Ann Underhill, a member of a large and prominent Oxford family. Thomas and Ann James had seven children, including a son called Francis.[199] Francis was the father of another Thomas James, who was a journeyman printer in Silver Street, in the parish of St. Olave, London. This younger Thomas James married Elinor Bankes and their daughter, Jane James, married Thomas Ilive, also a printer. Perhaps this was an arranged marriage between the two printing families.

Thomas and Jane Ilive's sons Abraham, Jacob and Isaac Ilive, were

Elinor James *c.* 1690. Unknown artist, oil on canvas, 126.8 × 103.5 cm. National
Portrait Gallery (NPG 5592).

printers like their forbears. Their grandmother, Elinor James née Bankes, was a Jacobite supporter and 'a notable printer and polemicist' in her own right. Elinor James 'wrote, printed and distributed broadsides and pamphlets addressing political, religious and commercial concerns'.[200] She had been arrested and confined in Newgate Prison for her published accusation that William III ruled illegitimately but, despite this, she continued to publish her controversial views. Paula McDowell writes that Elinor James was 'one of the most prolific and politically active women writers of the later Stuart period. A middle-class tradeswoman with a printing press in her own home, her works chronicling the national events of a tumultuous period are a unique resource for the recovery of popular female involvement in early modern political culture'.[201] It is exciting to discover that this determined woman would have been Elizabeth Ilive's great-grandmother. Abraham himself was the printer of several seditious pamphlets – a fact passed down in the family[202] – and was also known to have Jacobite sympathies. His brother Jacob Ilive was more well-known as a printer at the time and was the only son to inherit the family printing business from their mother Jane.[203]

Abraham, apparently, had two or three wives prior to marrying Elizabeth's mother Cecilia. Intriguingly, these marriages were made in the Fleet Prison[204] – possibly because Abraham may have been a Dissenter or perhaps because his first wife was actually still alive. Described as a printer of Aldgate, widower, he married Mary Phipps, widow on 6th March 1729.[205] Another marriage is less certain: Abraham Ilive, 'Hosier of Shoreditch', widower, married Elies Ball widow on 28th November 1731.[206] Information given at marriages conducted by clergymen resident in the Fleet Prison was likely to be inaccurate, as people tended to be married there because they had something to hide. Therefore, Abraham the printer may have deliberately said that he was a hosier in order to mislead someone.

The last record we can find is of Abraham Ilive, printer of St. George the Martyr, Southwark, widower, who married Elisabeth Chamberlin, widow, on 24th October 1737.[207] At the marriage to Elisabeth Chamberlin there seems to be some doubt as to whether Abraham's previous wife was actually dead and he was obliged to 'declare her death'.[208]

Abraham seemingly led a colourful life, involved as he was with the early days of London newspapers and working for the notorious William Rayner whose press was opposite the Kings Bench Prison. Abraham was also, on one occasion, persuaded to counterfeit American bills by a visitor from New Jersey but, after printing the paper money, Ilive informed on the man.[209]

The rather fantastical story told by Thomas Hamilton Ayliffe and his grand-daughter could indeed have a germ of truth, given the actual background of Abraham Ilive and Elinor James. Perhaps Thomas was brought up on tales of Jacobite supporters, handed down over generations, which he connected with his own family.

It is interesting to speculate that one person at Petworth House who may have been familiar with the name of the Ilive printers of Aldersgate was the tutor, Thomas Sockett. His father had been a stationer and bookseller in the same part of London, apprenticed in 1747. The Sockett family lived in Aldersgate Street when Thomas was born in 1777 – the year Abraham Ilive died.

Even if Thomas Sockett did make a connection with the Ilives of Aldersgate, he is unlikely to have made his thoughts public, out of respect for his employers and therefore Elizabeth's origins remained elusive for many years.

LEIGH LAWSON

Unknown artist, *Elizabeth Ilive*, oil on copper, 26 × 20 cm. Private collection, courtesy of Elinor Gallant and Jo Gallant.

Endnotes

1   *The Greville Memoirs 1814-1860* ed. Lytton Strachey and Roger Fulford, 8 vols; entry for May 1834.

2   *The Diary of Joseph Farington*, 9 October 1803, ed. Garlick and Macintyre, 1979, vol. VI p. 2140.

3   Wilfred Scawen Blunt, (quoting Elizabeth's grandson – his first cousin – Percy Wyndham, 13 July 1908) *My Diaries*, 2 volumes, Secker, London 1919, vol. 2, p. 206.

4   Petworth House Archives (hereafter PHA) 50 and London Metropolitan Archives, P89 MRY/008.

5   Somerset Record Office, DD/WY/199.

6   H. A. Wyndham, *A Family History 1688-1837*, OUP, 1950, p. 222.

7   Wyndham, p. 222.

8   Blunt, quoting Percy Wyndham, 13 July 1908.

9   This story seems to have arisen because of Thomas Hamilton Ayliffe's middle name.

10 Ozias Humphrey to Farington, 9 October 1803, vol.VI p. 2140.

11 Daniell to Farington, 27 March 1804, vol. VI p. 2280.

12 Dorset Record Office, *Western Times*, 1886.

13 *The Genealogy of the most Ancient and Noble Family of Wyndham... by William Radclyffe, Rouge Croix Pursuivant of Arms, 1819 and continued to the year 1821.*

14 'Thomas Ilive: Free by servitude from apothecary apprenticeship', MF 8206/3, London Metropolitan Archives.

15 Ilive, Thomas, Chemist, druggist, apothecary, male midwife, Portsmouth St., Lincolns Inn Field, *Holden's London Directory*, 1802.

16 Webb's *Apothecary Apprentices 1670-1800*; Society of Apothecaries Membership lists.

17 *Jackson's Oxford Journal*, 25 January 1777, p. 3.

18 Stationers' Company pension records, accessed on microfilm at the Bodleian Library.

19 Westminster Archives Centre, MS B1184, 189. *St. Clement Danes, Examinations Book, 1776-1779*. We are grateful to Jeremy Masters for the discovery of this document.

20 ibid.

21 ibid.

22 London Metropolitan Archives, P69/BOT1/A/001, St. Botolph Aldersgate, composite register.

23 Westminster Archives Centre, MS B1184, 189, *St. Clement Danes, Examinations Book, 1776-1779*.

24 London Metropolitan Archives, P69/BOT1/B/046/MS 01472/001 'Register of the Poor in the Parish Poor House', St. Botolph Aldersgate: City of London. We are grateful to Jeremy Masters for the discovery of this document.

25 *The Ayliffe Family as Collected by Ian Hamilton 1977*.

26 Probably Colonel Augustus Meade, 13th (Somerset) Regiment 1795; then 48th (Northampton) Regiment until 1812 when transferred to 91st (Argyllshire) Regiment of Foot. Served in the Peninsula 1812-14; wounded at Toulouse; brevet colonel 1811, retired 1818. www.napoloean-series.org. Died 1851, buried at All Souls Cemetery, Kensal Green with no headstone.

27 Somerset Record Office, DD/WY/199.

28 London Metropolitan Archives, P89/MRY1/008.

29 PHA 8658.

30 Elizabeth is named as Miss Ilive in the accounts for 1793, PHA 2233, and Mrs. Wyndham in the accounts for 1797, PHA 2237.

31 PHA 2230.

32 See Lydia Collins, 'George Seymour Crole a son of King George IV' in *Genealogists Magazine*, Vol. 21, No. 7, September 1984, pp. 228-233.

33 *Sussex Weekly Advertiser*, 1788-91.

34 PHA N15/A15 a-c.

35 PHA 3028.

36 PHA 8661.

37 West Sussex Record Office (hereafter WSRO) Par 149 1/1/1.

38 See P. Diday; translated by G. Whitley, *A treatise on syphilis in new-born children and infants at the breast*, London: The New Sydenham Society, 1859 and also Kevin Brown, *The Pox: The Life and Near Death of a Very Social Disease*, Sutton Publishing Ltd., 2006.

39   John Johnson ed. *Memoirs of the life and writings of William Hayley Esq. and of his son Thomas Alphonsus Hayley, the sculptor*, London 1823, 2 vols., WSRO Crookshank Collection 55 and 56. Vol. 1 p. 455.

40   Hayley Vol. 2 pp. 145-6; the painting titled *The Egremont Family*, is now No. 381 in C. H. Collins Baker Catalogue of the *Petworth Collection of Pictures*, London, 1920.

41   William Shakespeare, *A Midsummer Night's Dream*, Act II Scene III.

42   Farington Diary, 3 May 1797, vol. III, p. 833-4.

43   For example PHA 8059-8061.

44   PHA 8059, 8064.

45   PHA 5952.

46   William McCarthy *Anna Letitia Barbauld*, quoting Charlotte Yonge, Johns Hopkins University Press, Baltimore, p. 217.

47   Letitia Barbauld, *Lessons for Children from two to three years old*, London 1787, bought in 1803, PHA 5952.

48   E. V. Lucas edition, *The Letters of Charles Lamb*, *1935*, J.M. Dent vol. 1 p. 326

49   PHA 5952.

50   British Library *A Cabinet of Lilliput*, 10 vols., J. Harris, London, 1802.

51   PHA 8059.

52   PHA 8064.

53   ibid.

54   ibid.

55   PHA 2228.

56   PHA 2229, 2240.

57   PHA 2236.

58   PHA 2228, 2230, 2233, 2238, 2240, 2242.

59   PHA 8082.

60   ibid.

61   Royal Society of Arts (hereafter RSA) Minutes of the Committees 1795-96 Adelphi: Feb 4th 1796 Mechanics. Elizabeth's letter was edited slightly for publication in RSA *Transactions* 1796, 2295-8.

62   Blunt p. 206, 13 July 1908.

63   PHA 70, letter to the Earl from Samuel More in which he sends 'his best Respects to Mrs. Wyndham and all the Younger Branches' 23 Nov. 1797.

64   PHA 2236.

65 Arthur Young *Autobiography* ed. Matilda Betham-Edwards 1898, Smith, Elder and Co., London.

66 PHA 91.

67 PHA 2235.

68 RSA Minutes of the Committees 1795-96 Adelphi: Feb 4th 1796 Mechanics.

69 RSA PR/MC/101/10/1541.

70 RSA Minutes of the Committees 1795-96 Adelphi: Feb 4th 1796 Mechanics.

71 ibid.

72 RSA C10/147, PR/MC/101/10/1841.

73 William McCarthy, *Anna Letitia Barbauld*, Johns Hopkins University Press, Baltimore 2008, p. 499.

74 RSA PR/MC/101/10/1541.

75 PHA 12009.

76 PHA 6635, 8058 and 9271.

77 PHA 91.

78 *Annals of Agriculture* XXIX, 1797.

79 PHA 91.

80 ibid.

81 ibid.

82 *Annals of Agriculture* XVII, 1797, p. 324.

83 PHA 8142, 8059.

84 PHA 8059.

85 Quote from Parson Woodforde's diary Nov. 1800. James Woodforde *The Diary of a Country Parson 1758-1802*, OUP, 1978.

86 Hayley, Vol. 2 p. 127.

87 WSRO Par 202/1/1/3 Thomas Alphonso son of Mary Cockerell baptised 5 November 1780 at Walberton, West Sussex.

88 Devon Record Office 59/7/4/8a; Hayley vol. 2 pp. 127-9

89 Sheila Haines and Leigh Lawson *Poor Cottages & Proud Palaces*, Hastings Press, 2007.

90 Hayley p. 334.

91 PHA 1679.

92 PHA 8051.

93 Alison McCann, 'A Private Laboratory at Petworth House, West Sussex in the late 18th century', *Annals of Science*, 40 (1983), pp. 635-55.

94   PHA 91. See also John Claudius Loudon, *An encyclopaedia of gardening comprising the theory and practice etc etc*, Longman 1824, p. 161 note 731 – 'Hydrogen gas. A plant of the epilobium hirsutum, which was confined by [Joseph] Priestley in a receiver filled with inflammable air or hydrogen, consumed one third of its atmosphere and was still green. Hence Priestley inferred, that it serves as a vegetable food, and constitutes even the true and proper pabulum of the plant...'

95   PHA 8064.

96   British Library ADD MS 35129 f350.

97   PHA 8060.

98   PHA 2237-2239.

99   PHA 55.

100   PHA 1679.

101   PHA 91.

102   Farington Diary, 18 December 1798, vol. III, pp. 1113-4.

103   PHA 8064.

104   Farington Diary, 18 December 1798, vol. III, p. 1114.

105   PHA 2088.

106   PHA 8082, PHA 10643.

107   PHA 8064.

108   PHA 2239.

109   PHA 8661.

110   PHA 5951.

111   PHA 8656.

112   WSRO Par 149 1/1/5.

113   PHA 8656.

114   *Brighton Patriot*, 21 November 1837.

115   Dorset Record Office, *Western Times*, 1886.

116   PHA 14930.

117   Par 149 1/1/2.

118   PHA 4425.

119   PHA 2097.

120   PHA 10643.

121   PHA 4425.

122   PHA 12013 No. 177.

123   PHA 10643.

124   PHA 69.

125   PHA 10643 2/2.

126   Blunt, quoting Percy Wyndham, 13 July 1908.

127   Farington Diary, 9 October 1803 vol. VI 2140.

128   Daniell to Farington, 27 March 1804, Diary vol. VI, 2280-1.

129   PHA 12014.

130   PHA 8025.

131   PHA 7547.

132   ibid.

133   *The notebook of William Blake: photographic and typographic facsimile*; edited by David V. Erdman, Clarendon Press, 1973.

134   Frederick Tatham, *The Letters of William Blake, together with a life by Frederick Tatham*, ed Archibald G.B. Russell, Methuen and Co. Letter to Thomas Butts, 11 September 1811.

135   Hayley, vol. II p. 47.

136   WSRO QR/W643.

137   Milton *Paradise Lost*, Book One.

138   PHA 87.

139   PHA 8662.

140   Daniell to Farington, 27 March 1804. Diary vol. VI, p. 2281.

141   PHA uncatalogued box 1241.

142   Blunt, p. 206, 13 July 1908.

143   London Metropolitan Archives, DL/T/089/004.

144   PHA 7547.

145   PHA 11052.

146   Staffordshire County Record Office, D3794/13/1A and B.

147   *Morning Post*, 21 April 1817.

148   *Morning Post*, 8 October 1817.

149   *Morning Chronicle*, 17 August 1819.

150   PHA 12013. Tyler said it was 'quite a small house only two rooms on each floor, three in basement and attic'.

151   PHA 1088-1093.

152   PHA 12013.

153   Royal Academy, HU 6/47. Humphrey lodged with the Thomas family.

154   PHA 1089.

155   PHA 1090.

156   PHA 7547.

157   PHA H14/29.

158   ibid.

159   PHA 7547.

160   PHA 1090.

161   Staffordshire County Record Office, D3794/13/1A and B.

162   PHA 12018.

163   PHA 1090.

164   *Morning Post*, 2 January 1819.

165   PHA 7547.

166   ibid.

167   ibid.

168   ibid.

169   ibid.

170   PHA 11054 and *Morning Chronicle* 3 January 1823, 'On Monday night last, between eleven and twelve o'clock at her house, in Waterloo-place, the Countess of Egremont aged 53'.

171   PHA 2687.

172   Right Honourable Countess of Egremont buried 10 January 1823 aged 53 St. Decuman's burial register, Somerset Record Office 2/1/11.

173   Somerset Record Office, DD/WY Box 199.

174   PHA 7547.

175   PHA 12019.

176   ibid.

177   ibid.

178   PHA 7547.

179   PHA 4445.

180   PHA 7547.

181   ibid.

182   London Metropolitan Archives, MS/11936/494/1008259.

183   PHA 12020.

184   We are grateful to Anne Monk for telling us of the existence of this silverware.

185   PHA 7547.

186   *London Gazette*, Issue 18108, 15 February 1825.

187   PHA 7923.

188   PHA 59.

189   PHA 7923.

190   PHA 8641.

191   Burke, Sir Bernard, *A Genealogical and Heraldic Dictionary of the Peerage and Baronetage of the British Empire*, Eighteenth Edition 1856, Thirty-third Edition 1871 and Forty-fourth Edition, 1882.

192   Wyndham, H. A., *A Family History, 1688-1837: the Wyndhams of Somerset, Sussex and Wiltshire*, OUP, 1950.

193   *The London Stage*, Part 5 1776-1800 vol. 3, Schneider.

194   The National Archives, PROB 11/1398/334.

195   Correspondence with Leslie Tomas Miller, Madrid, 2014.

196   Baptism registers (1797-1815) of St. James, Spanish Place; Sardinian Embassy Chapel; St. Patrick's Catholic Chapel and Westminster St. Mary with thanks to Jeremy Masters for this information – see http://atavus.com.au/ilive.

197   Cliff Webb, Apothecary Apprentices 1670-1800.

198   E Rowe Mores: *A dissertation upon English typographical founders and founderies 1778*.

199   James, Thomas (1572/3-1629) 'librarian and religious controversialist' R. Julian Roberts, *Oxford Dictionary of National Biography*, OUP, 2004.

200   James [née Banckes], Elinor [Eleanor] (1644/5-1719), 'printer and polemicist' Paula McDowell, *Oxford Dictionary of National Biography*, OUP, 2004.

201   ibid.

202   *The Ayliffe Family as Collected by Ian Hamilton 1977*, published on the internet http://www.hamiltonewell.com.au/archives.

203   London Metropolitan Archives & Guildhall Libraries, MS 9052/44 will number 238.

204   Registers of Clandestine Marriages and of Baptisms in the Fleet Prison, Kings Bench Prison, the Mint and the May Fair Chapel. RG7.

205   ibid.

206   ibid.

207   ibid.

208   RG7 piece 303.

209   Pennsylvania Archives, 1739.

Timeline

1706   Abraham Ilive, Elizabeth's father, baptised at St. Botolph, Aldersgate, London.
1769   Elizabeth Ilive was said to have been born.
1777   Abraham Ilive, printer, died in Oxford.
        Mrs. Cecilia Ilive received pension from Stationers Company.
1778   Cecilia Ilive inmate of the parish workhouse of St. Botolph, Aldersgate.
c.1785 Elizabeth was supposed to have been only 15 years of age when she became the mistress of George O'Brien Wyndham, 3rd Earl of Egremont, who was 20 years her senior.
1787   George Wyndham Ilive, the first child of Elizabeth Ilive and the Earl of Egremont was born.
1789   Frances Wyndham Ilive, the second child, born.
1790   Henry Wyndham Ilive, the third child, born.
        Elizabeth Ilive appeared in the Petworth House Archives with the courtesy title Mrs. Wyndham.
1798   'Cesele Iliff' discharged from workhouse of St. Botolph, Aldersgate.
1792   Edward Wyndham Ilive, the fourth child, born 1792 died 1792.
        Mary Fox, daughter of the Earl and Eliza Fox born.
1793   William Wyndham Ilive, the fifth child, born 1793. William Hayley was William's godfather.
1794   William Wyndham Ilive died.
1795   Charlotte Wyndham Ilive, the sixth child, born 1795.
        Elizabeth submitted her design for an improved cross-bar lever to the Royal Society of Arts, London.
1796   Potato growing trials begun by Elizabeth at Petworth.
        Elizabeth won a Silver Medal from the RSA for her cross-bar lever.
        Charles Wyndham Ilive, the seventh child, born 1796.
1797   Elizabeth wrote a report of the potato trials for Arthur Young who published her article in the *Annals of Agriculture*.
        Laboratory for scientific experiments set up at Petworth House.

1798	Elizabeth visited the Orleans exhibition of paintings in London.
1800	Payment of Stationers Company pension ceased to be paid to Cecilia Ilive.
1802	Purchase of a swing cot for a baby.
	Marriage of Elizabeth and the Earl at the parish church of Petworth.
1803	Lady Elizabeth Wyndham, the eighth and only legitimate child, born and died soon afterwards.
	Elizabeth and the Earl separated, she went to live in London.
1805	Disagreements between Elizabeth and the Earl over finances.
	William Blake dedicated his painting *Satan Calling Up His Legions* to Elizabeth.
1807	The Earl bought Hurlingham House in Fulham, near London, as a home for Elizabeth.
1812	The Earl made a new will, making a settlement on Elizabeth and leaving Hurlingham House to her.
1815	Hurlingham needed repairs and was let.
1819	Elizabeth moved to Waterloo Place, London.
1822	Elizabeth died at home in Waterloo Place, end of December.
1823	January, Elizabeth's body taken to Watchet in Somerset, to be buried in the Wyndham family vault in the parish church of St. Decuman.
1837	George O'Brien Wyndham 3rd Earl of Egremont died.
1838	Thomas Hamilton Ayliffe and family emigrated to Australia.
1839	George, Henry and Charles acquired a Royal Licence to use the surname Wyndham instead of Wyndham Ilive.

Bibliography

PRIMARY SOURCES

British Library. Correspondence and Papers of Arthur Young, 1803-1820; database of local and provincial newspapers.

Dorset Record Office, *Western Times*.

London Metropolitan Archives: parish records of St. Marylebone; parish records of St. Botolph's without Aldersgate.

Oxford Record Office: indexes to registers of all parishes in the city of Oxford; parish register of St. Thomas, Oxford; microfilm of *Jackson's Oxford Journal*, 1777.

Royal Academy of Arts, Ozias Humphry Papers.

Royal Society for the encouragement of Arts, Manufactures and Commerce, *Transactions*; Minutes of the Committees.

Somerset Record Office, Wyndham Papers; St. Decuman's burial register.

Staffordshire and Stoke-on-Trent Archive Service, Shirley family, Earl Ferrers Papers.

Stationers' Company Records (accessed on microfilm at the Bodleian Library).

Will of Thomas Iliff of Dean's Yard, Westminster, clerk, 1803 The National Archives, PROB 11/1398/334.

West Sussex Record Office: parish registers of Petworth; parish registers of Walberton. Petworth House Archives, accessed via West Sussex Record Office.

SECONDARY SOURCES

Bacot, John *A treatise on syphilis in which the history, symptoms, and method of treating every form of that disease, are fully considered*, 1829.

Barbauld, Anna Letitia; *Lessons for Children from Two to Three years Old*, London, J. Johnson, 1787.

Baron, John *Life of Edward Jenner*, London, 1837.

Blake, William, *Notebook*, facsimile, ed. David V. Erdman, Oxford, 1973.

Blake, William, *Seen in My Vision, A descriptive catalogue of Pictures*, ed. Martin Myrone, Tate Publishing, 2009.

Blunt, Wilfred Scawen, *My Diaries*, 2 vols., Secker, 1919.

Brown, Kevin, *The Pox: The Life and Death of a very Social Disease*, Sutton, 2006.

Diday, P., *A treatise on syphilis in new-born children and infants at the breast*, translated by G. Whitley, London: The New Sydenham Society, 1859.

Farington, Joseph, *Diary*, ed. Kenneth Garlick and Angus Macintyre, Yale, 1979.

The Greville Memoirs 1814-1860, ed. Lytton Strachey and Roger Fulford, 8 vols.

Gilchrist, Alexander, *Life of William Blake*, J.M.Dent, 1863.

Iliff, William Tiffin, *The Monumental Inscriptions in The Old Churchyard of St. Mary, Newington, Surrey. Part 1. With Annotations.* London, privately printed, 1880.

Haines and Lawson, *Elizabeth Ilive Comes Alive: Petworth House Archives*, West Sussex History: Journal of the West Sussex Archives Society number 78, 2010.

Haines and Lawson, *Poor Cottages and Proud Palaces, The Life and Work of the Reverend Thomas Sockett of Petworth 1777-1859*, Hastings Press, 2007.

Hamilton, Ian, *The Ayliffe Family as Collected by Ian Hamilton 1977*, published on the internet http://www.hamiltonewell.com.au/archives.

Hayley, William, *Memoir of the life and writings of William Hayley, Esq., and of his son Thomas Alphonso Hayley, the sculptor.* 2 vols., London 1823, WSRO Crookshank Collection 55 and 56.

Howes and Roche, *Founder's London A-Z*, Friends of St. Bride Printing Library, 1998.

Masters, Jeremy, *'Mr. Ayliffe, Surgeon' and 'This Ingenious Lady' Uncovering the Origins of Thomas Hamilton Ayliffe and Elizabeth, the Countess of Egremont'* privately printed 2015 and published on the internet http://atavus.com.au/ilive/.

McCarthy, William, *Anna Letitia Barbauld; Voice of the Enlightenment*, Johns Hopkins, Baltimore, 2008.

McCann, Alison, *A Private Laboratory at Petworth House Sussex in the late 18th century*, Annals of Science, 40, 4 Nov., 1983.

Mores, Edward Rowe, *A Dissertation upon English Typographical Founders and Founderies*, 1778.

Oxford Dictionary of National Biography, Oxford University Press, 2004.

Radclyffe, William, *The Genealogy of the most Ancient and Noble Family of Wyndham* 1819, continued in 1821.

Rowell, Christopher, *Petworth, the People and the Place*, National Trust, 2012.

Webb, Cliff, *Apothecary Apprentices 1670-1800*, Society of Genealogists, 1996.

Woodford, James, *The Diary of a Country Parson 1758-1802*, Oxford University Press, 1978.

Wyndham, H. A. *A Family History 1688-1837*, Oxford University Press, 1950.

Young, Arthur, ed., *Annals of Agriculture and Other Useful Arts*, 1784-1815.

Index